P9-DDB-627

Group Piano-Teaching

YVONNE ENOCH

LONDON

OXFORD UNIVERSITY PRESS

NEW YORK TORONTO

1974

786.3 .
En64g

LIBRARY
ATLANTIC CHRISTIAN COLLEGE
WILSON, N. C.

Oxford University Press, Ely House, London W.1

GLASGOW   NEW YORK   TORONTO   MELBOURNE   WELLINGTON
CAPE TOWN   IBADAN   NAIROBI   DAR ES SALAAM   LUSAKA   ADDIS ABABA
DELHI   BOMBAY   CALCUTTA   MADRAS   KARACHI   LAHORE   DACCA
KUALA LUMPUR   SINGAPORE   HONG KONG   TOKYO

ISBN 0 19 318421 4

© Oxford University Press, 1974

*All rights reserved. No part of this publication may be reproduced,
stored in a retrieval system, or transmitted, in any form or by any means,
electronic, mechanical, photocopying, recording, or otherwise, without
the prior permission of Oxford University Press*

*Printed in Great Britain
by W & J Mackay Limited, Chatham*

'What is it to be a musician? Not to have the eyes bent on the notes, and play the piece laboriously to the end; not (supposing one happens to turn two pages instead of one) to get stuck and be unable to carry on. To be a musician is when in a new piece you can almost guess what is coming, when you know an old piece by heart—in a word, when you have music not only in your fingers, but in your head and heart too.'

Advice to Young Musicians

SCHUMANN

77- 2827

To Jim
without whose encouragement
I would never have started group teaching

Contents

Preface

In 1956, when I joined the staff of the Kent (then Rural) Music School, I was asked to develop a method of teaching the piano to groups of pupils which could be used by any teacher, and which was not dependent upon the use of any particular music or method of teaching the instrument.

Like so many others, I had never seen any instrumental group-teaching nor even read the few books that had been written on the subject, and I was not a little sceptical about the value of such teaching, or even its possibility. But the Kent Music School made no stipulations and in fact gave me opportunities for experiment that far exceeded my wildest hopes. I was allowed to start groups in any way I liked, keeping them for as long or as little as necessary, according to the success or failure of the particular experiment in hand. I started in a Secondary Modern School with seemingly no ideas and a lot of manuscript paper. Later I tried out countless ways of approaching the subject in all types of schools including a Girls' Borstal, and with adults. Each experiment added something of value to the next. I 'sat in' on primary school reading lessons in an attempt to review the more normal method of teaching notation, and even attended courses on string class-teaching. All these activities stimulated me to grapple with the challenge of the Piano Group, until at last, to my excitement, I realized that I no longer wished to teach pupils individually.

In 1967 I had the great good fortune to be awarded a Churchill Fellowship and I travelled to the USA and Canada for three months in order to observe piano class-teaching methods in these countries, where piano classes have flourished for many years.

This book is the outcome of those years of learning and experiment. I hope it will prove of value to all those who are teaching the piano to groups, and that it will help to convince the sceptical that it is worth trying.

It has been a challenge, but what a challenge!

I would like to acknowledge the advice and help given me in the writing of this book by the late Mervyn Bruxner and to thank Ella Grundy for making the typescript.

1 Planning the Group

Thousands of children start to learn to play the piano each year. The eagerness with which they approach their first lessons is often short-lived. The piano is a lonely instrument, and it may be that the lack of stimulus derived from learning with others of the same age accounts in part for the enormous fall-out of pupils after a few years. The group-lesson combats this loneliness, and to a certain extent compensates the pianist for the lack of communal music-making so much enjoyed by those who play orchestral instruments.

To be capable musicians, besides understanding the musical content of the pieces they play, children should be really good sight-readers; be able to transpose at sight; accompany well and have sufficient knowledge of keyboard harmony to enable them to add a bass part to a melody. Since enthusiasm is catching, all these things can be taught more readily in the group situation.

In the group, children learn from one another, discover new things together, play together and learn to criticize and be criticized constructively. The competitive spirit, and the fact that the success of the group as a whole is dependent on the success of each individual in it, leads to the necessity for practice by each member of the group. This hastens progress and in consequence the interest in playing.

The group-lesson is never frightening, as the individual lesson can sometimes be, especially for the very shy and the younger child. It is a consolation to many who see their own faults repeated by others in the group.

Because the group soon discovers that the success of each lesson largely depends on the work done by each individual, you will rarely experience the dreariness of teaching pupils who do not practise. You can in turn be stimulated by the excitement engendered by the group.

HOW MANY PIANOS?

The greatest difficulty in group-teaching is to keep the lesson directed to the group as a whole, and not to let it degenerate into the 'five-minute' lesson in which one child at a time has all your attention at the piano, while the remainder of the group do something else.

In America one piano or electronic-keyboard is usually available at the lesson for each member of the group as well as for the teacher. But one of the main assets of the group-lesson is that by developing the critical faculties of the group, the individuals become involved in each other's playing. This also teaches them to criticize and to listen more acutely to their own performances. If all the children play together throughout most of each lesson, this critical faculty is not developed and the ability to listen is diminished; children are prevented from learning from one another and from sharing in each other's experiments with sounds.

The teacher, in fact, gives an individual lesson, eliminating the essential qualities and benefits of the group-lesson. You should therefore not use more than two pianos.

To teach the piano to groups of children needs quite a different approach from teaching individuals.

ENROLMENT

There are many schools of thought concerning the advisability of testing children's musical potential before enrolment for individual lessons. If the list of pupils wanting lessons is very long and entails setting up a waiting-list, it would presumably be a sensible measure to take. But what form should these tests take? The vital prerequisites for any pianist-musician are good aural perception—this means the ability to distinguish high notes from low ones—and preferably the ability to sing notes correctly; an inborn rhythmic sense; and hands that are neither deformed in any way, nor impossibly small.

I have known children who would have been turned down on all these counts had they been so tested—children who apparently were unable to hear differences of pitch and who certainly could not have sung a note in tune; some unable to walk or clap rhythmically, and those too with pathetically thin fingers or small hands without stretch. By copying others in a group and learning from them, many if not most of these seemingly unpromising pupils have learnt to pitch correctly, reproduce rhythms accurately, and in spite of poor hands have achieved surprising results, and it seems only right that *all* children should be given a chance to 'have a go' if they really want to. Children can help one another so much if they learn together, and much of your time can be saved by teaching notation and so on to six pupils at a time instead of to one after the other. The case of the adult pupil is different; he should certainly have aural and rhythm tests.

Ideally, children should be introduced to music much as they are to speech, by listening to it long before they have any conception of its meaning. The child who develops most musically is often the one whose parents have sung to him during his infancy. Singing and discovering sounds should be a part of every child's daily life.

All music-teaching should start at latest by Primary School age. Many children will wish to learn to play the piano before then. Owing to the slow rate of progress that can be made with such young children, it is usually better not to recruit children to the piano-group until they are aged eight. Children younger than this find it difficult to learn in the group situation, and are often no further advanced by the age of nine than they would have been had they started when older. Very young children do better when taught individually for the first few years, joining a group when old enough to enjoy it.

When you sort children into groups, try to keep the eight-year-olds together and mix the nine- and ten-year-olds; there is often a gap in the speed at which children can learn between the ages of eight and nine. Children should be grouped according to their intelligence, rather than by their musical potential.

It is always better to start with a minimum of two groups of six pupils each. You can then change children round according to their mental abilities; only later according to their musical potential. It may take several changes and half a term to sort pupils out. There is no reason, however, why two groups, once established, should progress at the same rate; each group must work as an entity in itself and at the speed at which it is able to assimilate the matter presented to it.

HOW MANY LESSONS AND HOW LONG?

Although every teacher of whatever instrument will argue that progress will be quicker and last longer when pupils are able to have two lessons per week rather than one, it is an even greater necessity for the piano group who will have the use of, at most, two instruments. Where two lessons a week are given, it is better if they are on different days, especially in the first term, but it is not long before children will have gained sufficient knowledge to enable them to have the two lessons, with a break in between them, on the same day: one lesson will deal mostly with pieces; the other will be concerned with technique and musicianship. At present many teachers feel that musicianship cannot be undertaken until much later in the musical education of the pupil, but, as will be seen in later chapters, it can and should be started at the very beginning. Young children are unable to concentrate over too great a period and their aural awareness in particular cannot be sustained for long; a forty-minute lesson is a good length.

The situation is different for the adult pupil. If a pupil is not taken privately by the teacher in his or her own home, teachers are expected to conform to the rules set out by the local Evening Institutes who mostly still expect the piano-group to be treated in the same manner as the geography or mathematics class, insisting on a two-hour period with a minimum (no maximum) number of ten to twelve students. It is to be hoped that more education authorities will become enlightened, and will understand that the adult student who has had a full working day before attending the Institute is already tired, and in addition is wholly unaccustomed to using his ears as well as his fingers in the specialized manner necessary to learn to play a musical instrument. It would be more helpful to divide the group into two and so to be able to demand complete concentration from the pupils during a forty-minute period. A further twenty-minute period with all the students together would benefit all, but two pianos would be essential. It can be argued that teachers are already able to carry this out, letting half the class read or do what they like while attention is given to the other half. But in doing this, pupils are being encouraged to allow non-musical matters to enter the classroom and so to destroy in part the concentration of those being taught, as well as encouraging those waiting for their

lesson to let music become a background noise over which
they read.

EQUIPMENT

It is essential to have (1) a piano in good working order that
is tuned regularly to British standard pitch, (2) an adjustable
stool (these need not be the expensive revolving variety; a
school model having three possible variations of height is
quite adequate), (3) tables or desks at which pupils may
sit, (4) hard chairs, (5) one plastic dummy-keyboard with
raised black keys for each pupil, (6) a footstool for young
pupils (this can be a simple piece of wood on a wedge-stand
that any parent or school caretaker could easily knock up),
and (7) a blackboard, ruled for music if possible.

There are many types of dummy-keyboards on the
market; the cheapest, made of cardboard, are not really
satisfactory, for children have to look at their hands the
whole time in order to see which notes they are 'playing'
and so a bad habit is formed at the start. Much more
expensive dummy-keyboards having simulated piano-action
are also available. As good teachers make their pupils
depress the keys in specific ways in order to produce variety
of tone, this type of keyboard unfortunately encourages the
pupil to play every note with the same touch, since he
cannot judge the quality of sound. They are also expensive
and cannot be carried round by the teacher in any quantity
easily. The latest electronic keyboards, also having piano
key-action, find their place more readily in the aural and
keyboard-harmony class, and as a rule are not recommended
for use with the piano-group. Quite the best to use are the
plastic keyboards* with raised black keys and a division
between the white keys which make it easy for the child to

* Available from Banks Ltd. of York, or Mills Music Ltd., London.

feel his way about without having to look down at his hands. Each keyboard has a compass of two octaves, and one keyboard interlocks with another to make any length needed. Dummy-keyboards will only be used for a short time during the first term.

Children will each need a copy of the music being taught, a notebook, and a manuscript book. You will find charts of the music for use at the lesson helpful. These can be bought ready ruled with four staves to a page, and you can write on them easily and quickly if you use a thick felt pen or magic marker.

CLASSROOM ARRANGEMENT

Children should be kept in as close-knit a group as possible. The more they are spread out, the harder will it be for you to keep them under complete surveillance, so vitally necessary, especially in the early stages. The piano should be placed so that the player has his back to the group. This is important, for young children can easily be distracted if they face the group, and the group must be able to criticize the posture of the pianist. The charts should be placed where they can be seen directly by all the children, and you should position yourself alongside the charts to which you can point easily and at the same time see the hands of each child, whether sitting at tables or playing the piano.

PREPARATION

(a) *The Teacher*. Thorough preparation of each lesson is essential. No longer are you able to sit back and let the teaching take shape as the lesson progresses according to the instant necessities of one child. You must know exactly what you aim to do with each group, and the demands you are to make on each individual, while at the same time being elastic enough to drop all you have prepared if the situation warrants it. If you have a large number of groups you may find it easier in preparing the work to make a stencil of the teaching activities which recur.

(b) *Practising*. Some dedicated teachers do not insist on their group pupils having any facilities for individual practice. Though in some instances this may still lead to the purchase of pianos by those who have none, in most cases it creates great frustration on the part of the pupil whose progress is of necessity very slow; many stop learning, and a great deal of extra patience and tenacity is needed by the teacher who has to supervise the practising at the lesson. If a group has a mixture of pupils, some able and some not able to practise at home, it leads to an impossible situation where either those who practise are kept back in order to help those who do not, or those who do not are left floundering while the rest of the group progress beyond them. Either way it leads to the break-up of the group.

Every child should practise daily, and parents of children must be told that a small amount of practice *every* day is far better than a longer stretch once or twice a week. Sometimes children who have no piano of their own make an arrangement with a friend or neighbour to use theirs, which is usually satisfactory. Less satisfactory is an arrangement for a child to practise at school, where many interruptions of one kind or another prevent proper concentration; also, the child is unable to work during school holidays. It also means that the child who practises for a prescribed time at school has no opportunity to 'doodle' at the piano, to discover things for himself or to play for the pure joy of doing so. Some firms will hire pianos to new pupils; this gives parents a chance to see whether their children have any aptitude for the instrument and are likely to continue to learn, before facing the heavy outlay entailed by the purchase of a piano. In most cases firms which hire pianos will agree to sell a piano after this hiring period, on hire-purchase terms.

REPORTS

Reports should be issued to the parents of each child taking lessons at least twice a year. They should be to the point, and helpful. If hand positions are bad in any way, knowledge of notation poor, or there are other difficulties, these should be mentioned so that the parent has some idea of what to watch in order to speed progress in the future.

FEES

In those counties whose Local Education Authorities provide instrumental classes free to school children, part-time teachers are paid an hourly flat-rate. Those teachers who, seeing so many children being taught at one and the same time, fear that the source of their income is in jeopardy, should remember that most Authorities limit free tuition to group-learning, which in its turn is often limited to a two-year period. Pupils wishing to have further lessons must pay and arrange these with local teachers. The teacher who has the courage to tackle group-teaching will benefit by having a ready-made source of pupils from which to draw every year.

While the arrangement of free tuition is not ideal, for one values most that which costs one dear, it does mean that every child has an opportunity of finding out whether he has any talent at all, and whether he really wants to learn. Many children continue with their studies who might never have started if such a scheme were not in operation.

If teachers charge their group-pupils a third of the fee usually made to individual pupils, they can earn more in less teaching time. The group-pupil will also gain by paying only two-thirds of the individual fee for two group-lessons a week.

2 The First Lessons

Sit the children down at the tables on which you have put a dummy-keyboard ready for each one. Ask the children to look at the keyboards and to tell you whether they notice any pattern of the keys. Most will be able to tell you pretty quickly that the black keys are grouped in twos and threes.

Show the group how the right-hand fingers are numbered, getting them to hold up whichever one you call out. This must take as little time as possible; prepare the children to think and react quickly right from the start. Do this with the left hand as well, but as you are facing the group, use the opposite hand yourself.

Now get the children to stand up and show them how to 'mark time'. Using any rhyme whose words fit into a regular pulse without subdivisions, such as Ex. 1 (children's names can also be used: Ex. 2), make the children say the words while marking time with their feet; set the rhythm yourself, keeping them all together.

Ex. 1

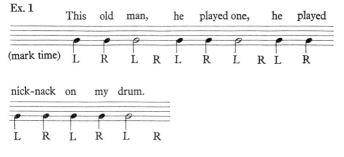

Ex. 2

Anne and John,   Sue   and Tom,   Jane,   Tim,   Pam and   Jim.

L   R   L R L   R   L R L   R L R L   R   L   R

Now ask the group if any whole word had more than one 'walk'. You may have to repeat the process several times, but after the second attempt usually one child will notice that you walk twice on 'man' and the others will follow with 'one' and 'drum'. From this exercise you establish that music is made up of notes of different lengths.

Get the children up to the piano all together so that they can watch one another. Using any three adjacent fingers and the three black keys, ask them each to make up a tune to the words already used keeping to the same rhythm. When they have all done this, tell them to make up another tune at home. As they have no knowledge of notation at this stage, some other means of indicating the tune must be devised, and a simple way is to write a straight line; a cross below this line will represent the lowest black key, a cross on the line the middle black key, and a cross above the line the highest black key, so that a tune may be represented like this:—

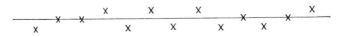

It is important that the children should be made to write their tunes down, for you want them to (a) experiment at home and (b) be able to remember their own tune even after hearing five other versions at the next lesson!

You must tell the children that they may start on any of the three notes they like, that they can move by 'step' to another note, 'skip' from the bottom to the top note, or vice versa, or repeat a note. This will suggest to children that

you have to look at the 'shape' of music, and will pave the
way for the teaching of sight-reading later. This use of the
black keys has a dual purpose, for it makes the children play
towards the back of the piano, keeping the wrists up and the
thumbs well over the keys—a hand position often difficult
to achieve in the early stages.

Now teach them their first three notes. I like to teach D
in the Treble and G and A in the Bass, for these are obviously
easy to find:

Ex. 3

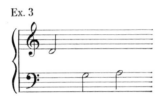

They are also the tonic and dominant of the keys of G and
D, and can be used to make very simple basic accompaniments for songs. As these are also the favourite keys of
violinists and recorder players, instrumentalists can be
invited to play with the pianists at the very earliest stages of
the pianist's career.

The use of these three notes to start with will also compel
the eye of the child to travel across both staves right from
the beginning; with the use of other notes, the eye is trained
initially to look along each stave separately.

Whichever notes you decide to use, it is easier to introduce them to the children while they sit at their tables,
using the dummy-keyboards. You can then see very rapidly
if each has understood what is being taught.

At the same time that the notes on the keyboard are
being taught, show also their position on the staves. At this
stage clefs, bar-lines, time-signatures, and note-values need
not be explained. Indeed all explanations must be kept to
the minimum possible, letting the children learn these

things as they proceed, through your casual and then constant mention of them. The child will remember most what he discovers for himself and you must at all costs have sufficient patience to allow this natural growth to develop

As soon as the children have understood the positioning of the notes on the keyboard, get them up to the piano again and make each of them 'spell' a word on the keyboard in turn—Add, Dad, Ada, Gag, Dada, Gad, singing the letter names as they play, or in the case where other notes than these are taught, the words made up from these letter names. Never correct the children yourself. Involve all the children together and ask them whether a word was correctly 'spelled' or not, and should any child say that something was wrong, do not question this decision but ask that child to make the correction. In this way children will learn to watch, listen, and think, and begin to criticize one another. Even if a criticism at this stage is incorrect, let it go by, asking another child if the correction made was accurate, so that children themselves correct each other, thus learning from one another. Unfortunately for your ego, children learn far more easily and quickly from one another than they ever will from you; pupils should be encouraged to help one another.

Now teach the children their first piece. While they sit at the tables, get them to look at your chart and 'spell' and sing the names of the notes as you point to them. If there is a minim in the piece simply sing the name of the note and add the count thus—'G-two', and at the end of the piece make sure that the last beat is held for its full length. So again if it is a minim sing 'D-two-off', pointing at the same time to the double bar at the end of the piece.

Children must learn all there is to know from every piece given to them, and this cannot be started too early, so it is important that they be taught to observe *all* that is written on the page. Ask the children what difference *they*

see between the positioning of notes on the stave, so that
they will establish this themselves. Ask also why you
counted 'G-two' to the minim; someone will tell you that
while the other notes are 'filled in' this one is open. Also let
them find out why at the end you said 'D-two-off'. For this
you may have to point to the bar-line after the first minim,
and then to the double bar, but do no more than point. It
is important that all the note-naming of the pieces should
be strictly in the rhythm of the notes *always*. This teaches
notes and rhythm together. Now let one child play this
'piece' at the piano, the others playing on the dummy-
keyboards.

Walking Tune

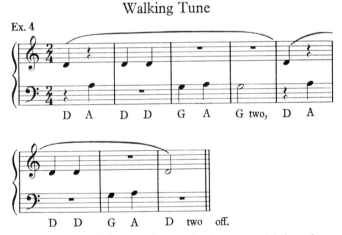

It is not possible to make much of a tune with just three
notes, but it will not harm the children to try to sing them
to the note-names as they play; children will begin to hear
the notes they see. Watch all the children as they play,
making sure that the correct fingers are used all the time
and that they watch the chart, *not* their fingers. To make
sure of this, only the child at the piano should have a copy
of the music. If the children sitting at tables are allowed to

use their own copies instead of looking at the chart, you will be unable to see whether each child is looking at the music or at his fingers. Each child should play the piece at the piano (children may on occasion play 2 or 3 together at the keyboard).

At this stage make no attempt to get good posture or finger and hand positions. Children have come to their first lesson eager to play the piano, and this they must do as soon as possible. It is also essential that they have a 'piece' to play which is easily within their capabilities and can be played to parents at home. To tell a child to make a beautiful sound is useless until he knows that it is possible to vary sounds on the piano and that it is easy to make very ugly sounds, so defer this for a lesson or two. Capture the child's enthusiasm first. This is done most easily at the very first lesson; if not achieved then, the chance may be lost for ever.

It is vitally important that you are sure the whole group has understood what has been done. Repetition in the early days of piano playing is important, particularly with children who may not be quick to grasp new things. If you are satisfied that all is well understood, and more lesson time is left, teach the group to sing a song whose accompaniment you will introduce at the next lesson. See Ex. 5 and Ex. 6, pages 19 and 20.

Tell the children what you want them to practise: give them one or two more pieces to learn by themselves, making sure that there is nothing new in any of them. Write what you have told the children very quickly and concisely in each child's notebook, so that parents know what work is to be done. You should also write down the amount of practising that should be done each day. I tell children that they should practise ten minutes every day, except Sunday. If the practice is good this is sufficient to start with; this is the time to explain to parents the importance of practising a little every day instead of a lot once a week.

I have also found parents who, in their determination to get their children on, make them practise up to one hour a day, though how they could occupy this time I have yet to discover. This must of course be stopped forthwith!

LESSON 2

It is most important to hear all the children play everything that you did at the last lesson and the work you set them to do on their own. The children will have practised this so it will not take long to hear each child individually. If you have prepared your lesson well, you will know exactly what you want each child to do. Having got them seated at their keyboards, test the children very quickly with the numbers of the fingers of each hand, and get them to show you on their keyboards where to find the three notes you have taught them. Now make all the children watch the charts and 'spell' the names of the notes of the first piece they learnt, in the rhythm of the tune. This will be spelt out as in Ex. 4 (see page 15).

It is up to you to establish the beat. If you can click your fingers at the speed at which you want the children to play this will suffice, otherwise you will have to count, and as children are as yet unaware that there could be several beats in a bar, counting can be confusing. The tick of a metronome and the tapping of a ruler or pencil are harsh unmusical sounds and should also be avoided if possible. You could, if you wished, count in French time-names out loud, but in no circumstances should you explain what you are doing nor *continue* to do it. Children will soon grasp what is happening. Let each child in turn play the piece at the piano. For the first four times let the others play at the same time on their keyboards—this concentrated repetition all helps to establish fundamentals. While the last two children play, the others should be told to listen to see whether the notes and rhythm are played correctly. All through the life of a group it is important to get the child who makes a criticism to justify it, making the correction himself; this should be started now. If this is not done, children will tend to make criticisms which they think you are expecting, without making sure of their facts first.

Be certain at this lesson to hear the tunes the children made up. Do not worry if they are similar one to the other. One child will often copy another at first; it may take a little time before the children have sufficient confidence to make up different tunes. Encourage them to make up other tunes to the same words and rhythm, this time using all five black keys, and using a wider range of the keyboard.

If you taught the children the words and tune of a song, to which you have written an accompaniment using just the few notes they know, refresh their memories and get them to sing it all together. Take no notice if some of the children are not able to sing in tune—never pinpoint this disability in any way. Sing the song again, but this time make the children 'walk the beats' as they did for 'This Old Man'. While still walking make them read the notes of the accompaniment. At this stage it is easier if the accompaniment is written mostly in crotchets, so that the pulse of the music is felt all through.

Sit the children and let them play the accompaniment on their keyboards, two only taking it in turn to play the piano. (The others should play it at another lesson.) Watch all the children while this is being done; you will soon see which one can play it easily and rhythmically. Sing the song again, still walking the beats and clapping the rhythm as it is sung. Choose the safest player and let him play while the rest of the class sing. Never let a mistake in the accompaniment be corrected. If the player loses his nerve and gets confused, see that he at least plays the last note with the

Oh dear, what can the matter be?

John - nie's so long at the fair!

L   R   L   R

Strawberry Fair

Ex. 6

Voice or Recorder

Moderato

As I was go-ing to Straw-ber-ry fair,

Piano

(walking)   L   R   L   R

Sing - ing, sing - ing but - ter - cups and dai - sies, I

L   R   L   R

met a mai - den tak -ing her ware, fol - de-

L   R   (etc.)

- dee: Her eyes were blue and gol- den her hair As

she went down to Straw - ber – ry fair,

Ri - fol, ri – fol tol – de-rid- dle - i' – do,

Ri – fol, ri – fol tol – de – rid- dle - de.

singers. In this way the art of accompanying is born. Let the children experiment and find out for themselves what happens if the accompanist repeats notes, stops and restarts, or even hesitates, and so loses the beat, while the singers continue with their song. They may need help in order to 'catch up' when mistakes are made, but it will not be long before they are able to follow the song, making adjustments themselves for any errors that occur.

Group the children round the piano and very briefly show how the hammers hit the strings when the key is depressed. Show also that the speed at which the hammer moves is determined by the speed at which the finger is used, and that the slowest movement of the hammer produces the softest sound. A very brief demonstration of the effect of the uses of the soft and sustaining pedals can be made, but do not go into lengthy details—all this will be taken care of when the necessity for the use of the pedal arises much later on. Little time will now be left for more new work, so set the children some pieces to practise that present no new difficulties. It is better not to set too much now, for time will have to be made at the next lesson to hear it. Nothing is more disheartening than to prepare work that is not heard at all.

LESSON 3

Start the lesson with the song, first spelling the notes of the accompaniment all together in the rhythm of the notes. Always try to make the children sing the names of the notes. No time should be taken to get this accurate; intonation will improve as they accustom themselves to the sounds of the notes. This will stand them in good stead in later years when they wish to sight-sing or mentally hear an unplayed work. *The voice is the most useful instrument and the most instructive one we possess and should be in constant use in all manner of music-making.*

There is no necessity now to walk the beats unless children have found it difficult to sustain a regular beat with their feet while singing the melody. Let two children play in turn while the others sing, making sure that the players are not the same children who played this accompaniment at the previous lesson. Two other short pieces can be played by other children, spelling and singing the notes first. Although all the children must play as much as possible at each lesson, not every piece will be played by every child. Those who miss a piece one lesson may play it at the next.

Correct posture and hand positions should be attended to now before bad habits set in. Show children how to sit at the correct height so that the arms slope gently down from shoulder to wrist, the latter being on a level with the keys. The moment the arm looks straight from the shoulder, or rises from the elbow, the posture no longer flows from shoulder to finger. In the former position the pupil is sitting too high; in the latter too low. Children seem to feel safer if they sit near to the keyboard but they must be encouraged to sit back from it. While a straight back is essential, it is equally bad for the child to sit like a ramrod—he should lean a little forward towards the keys. Pupils should be shown how to hold their arms up by the upper arm muscles, thus allowing the forearm complete freedom of movement and preventing stiffness in the fingers. It is essential to balance the body securely; small children unable to touch the floor with their feet should rest them on paper-covered books or on a foot rest.

To obtain good hand positions make each child hold a solid rubber ball (the size of a tennis ball). If this is held firmly in the palm of the hand with the fingers and thumb well round it, the child will be able first to see the shape made by his hand—top and bottom—especially noticing how the fingers curve round the ball. Holding the other hand just below the ball, the child should be made to release the ball, place the fingers on the keyboard, and spread them out one finger to a key. A good hand position is obtained. Make the child pick the ball up again, hold it with the 2nd finger and thumb, and press hard, remembering to keep the finger curved. This should be done with each finger in turn.

The piano is an awkward instrument in that the hand can never be seen from the front when playing. A 'seen' and 'felt' position can more readily be reproduced than an 'explained' one. These exercises must be done by each hand in turn with all the pupils together. When illustrating movements on a dummy-keyboard, every time you face the group you must be sure to use the opposite hand to that used by the children; if you do not do this, they will see your movements going in the reverse direction to their own and may get confused.

At this stage children must be told to keep their nails short and why it is necessary that they should do so. I start each lesson with a nail inspection. (Just telling children is not sufficient—you have to keep on about it!) For the rest of the term questions on posture should be asked of the children as soon as they sit at their tables. Do not take too much time over posture and hand positions at this lesson—at each subsequent lesson you can reinforce what you have already said.

Leave sufficient time to hear the children's latest black-key tunes, this time letting them try transposing them first on to the white keys to the left of the black ones (F, G, and A); then on to those to the right of the black keys, (G, A, and B). This will help them to understand that the same tunes may be played at different pitches. If there is time, hear another piece and spell the notes of a new one to be learnt by the children for the next lesson.

LIBRARY
ATLANTIC CHRISTIAN COLLEGE
WILSON, N. C.

77- 2827

$\mathcal{3}$ The First Term

Continue the lessons according to the pattern already outlined, and increasing the amount of knowledge very gradually.

Try to make children learn notation by 'instant recognition', introducing one new note at a time until its position on the stave and its name is familiar; do not teach them mnemonic sentences for the lines and spaces. The art of sight-reading depends upon the player's ability to look along and absorb the contents of a line *horizontally*, observing the movement of tunes by interval. But if you allow a child to count from the bottom upwards in order to find a note, this teaches him to think in a perpendicular direction. It is quite easy at a first lesson to make children sight-read a tune that moves by step or repetition of a note, so long as the note on which the tune starts is known by the child. Time permitting, it is a useful exercise to undertake and quite exhilarating for the child.

Time must also be found during the first few lessons to give each child a simple ear test sufficient to find out whether he has the ability to distinguish between 'high' and 'low' and the direction of high and low on the keyboard. Again, do not tell the child whether he is right or wrong, and in this instance do not ask the others to make a correction. Inability to hear correctly will not be helped by criticism; indeed criticism at this stage, especially by classmates, may set up a nervous reaction.

Every piece that is taught should be chosen for a specific teaching point as well as for appeal, not for the latter alone.

Music is the art of playing with sound, so the use of some dynamics should be introduced with the very earliest pieces. To tell a child to 'put the expression in' after he has learnt the notes and rhythm of a piece is like baking a cake and adding the fruit and the flavouring afterwards. As I said earlier, children will copy each other. They will also copy you (your faults as well, so be careful!). Play to them frequently to illustrate your teaching points, and show them what variety of tone can be produced from the piano. Do not over-indulge yourself—*short* illustrations will suffice. Bearing in mind the axiom of teaching sound before sight (this applies to notation and nearly everything else in music), introduce the use of dynamics by using known phenomena such as 'An Echo' to present forte and piano, or a sentence having a climax at the end to suggest a crescendo. A very good use of words to illustrate this is:*

'Strutting, strutting, strutting hen, You make noise enough for ten.'

If said with conviction by the group, the crescendo will readily display itself. The group can make up a tune for this; it can then be played in turn, those not playing listening to see if a crescendo has indeed been achieved:

Strutting Hen

Ex. 7

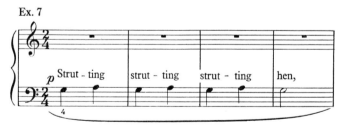

* Margaret and Mary Donington, *The Aural Background to the Pianist Musician* (London, Stainer & Bell).

If the tune in Ex. 7 is used, it will also serve to introduce legato playing from one hand to the other, and from the 4th to 3rd fingers of the left hand. Most children find this difficult to do at first. The following pencil exercise will help to overcome the difficulty. Make each child hold a pencil between the right-hand thumb and the 2nd finger so that the pencil rests across the thumb. Keeping the group rhythmically together, make the children 'play' from the 2nd to 3rd fingers; from the 3rd to 4th fingers; and lastly from the 4th to 5th fingers. Make them do this with the left hand as well. Care must be taken to see that children always play on the tips of their fingers. Should a child drop the pencil, ask the group why this happened, dropping it yourself for them to see and letting them do likewise. It is almost certain that at least one child will be able to tell you that one finger was not held until the other replaced it. Once this is seen, it can readily be applied to holding one finger down on a note until the next finger plays. If by chance nobody can give the reason, do not labour it, leave it without explanation and return to it on another occasion.

The more a child can learn about a piece before he begins to play it the better, and the more he knows about music generally the quicker will he learn to play his pieces. The very first pieces must have something to teach besides notes and rhythm. Ask a group what they notice about their piece. If you have made a chart of this piece and all the group are looking at it, one may tell you that the 'sticks' are not all the same length! This may be your bad writing, but no matter, the main thing is that a child noticed something and he should be praised for it. If you have chosen to teach them an Echo tune another child may notice the pattern of the rhythm, another the pattern of the tune, and yet another that the tune is repeated in the second phrase but that it starts on a different note:

An Echo Tune

You may have to help the group by asking the right question—'What about the length [time value] of the notes?', etc.—in order to get things going. In some pieces the second phrase may be an inversion of the first; in longer pieces the 1st and 3rd phrases may be identical; whatever the construction do let them do the actual discovering for themselves. Italian terms should be used straight away; pupils will remember the meanings of the few that will confront them at this stage; it will save their having to learn pages of them later. It is better for children to see music complete in every detail.

You must try to teach each new thing once only. To talk about a 'two-beat note' and then reintroduce it as a minim involves re-learning and can cause confusion; it also saves time and energy both for the children and for you if something is learnt correctly the first time.

When teaching a new rhythm, introduce it through something already known; base all teaching on going from the known to the unknown. Children should be able to sing and walk the beats of 'Nuts in May' and recognize the three beats on the word 'May' and on each syllable of 'morning'; older pupils may use 'Silent Night' or some other well-known tune:

Nuts in May

Ex. 9

The introduction of quavers, which should not be taken until well on into the first term, can more readily be understood if a tune such as 'Simple Simon' be taught first as a tune written in crotchets, subsequently in quavers:

Simple Simon

Ex. 10 a)

to the fair,_____ Said Sim-ple Si-mon

to the pie-man, "Let me taste your ware"._____

b)

Sim-ple Si-mon met a pie-man go-ing to the fair,___ Said

Sim-ple Si-mon to the pie-man, "Let me taste your ware".

If the beat is walked at the same speed in each case it will not be difficult for children to see that there are twice as many notes to each beat in the second version as there were in the first, and that the second version will therefore be played twice as fast as the first.

The teaching of touch, and indeed of most technical matters, is peculiar to each teacher and you should present collectively to the group the method you use in teaching individual pupils.

If children are to become really good sight-readers and are to acquire a facility to transpose, a thorough knowledge of all the keys is a vital prerequisite. It would be an impossible task to expect children to be able to play all the major scales, let alone the minor ones, during the first term of lessons. Scales have a complicated note pattern as well as a complicated finger pattern. In order to overcome this difficulty break the scales up into tetrachords, teaching the children to play these with one hand only to start with. If the fingers 1–4 are used *throughout*, only the note pattern has to be thought of. Tetrachords should be introduced at about the eighth lesson. Get the group to stand round the piano as you play the one beginning on C with the right hand:

Ex. 11

Keep the children standing at the piano, and let them copy what you have just played. They will not find this difficult and will quickly be able to play the tetrachord starting on G. Tell them now to play one starting on D. It may take a little time before any child plays F sharp, but be patient and on no account show them what to do. It is a good thing to make the children sing the tetrachord starting on G, followed by that starting on D, and try by singing to find which note is different from the one they play. They will easily discover that the third note is wrong, but will not know how to correct it, and in their attempts to make it sound sharper I have had many children bang out F, hoping that by playing it louder the pitch will rise! At this point you must be very alert, for a child may play the F sharp accidentally, or more rarely deliberately. Either way you must point it out, get the child to repeat what he has done, make the whole group sing it and become aware of its correctness. All the group must now play it and experiment immediately with the tetrachord starting on A. Set these four to be practised so that the children have no difficulty in playing them.

As soon as these are known, the group should discover the distance between each successive tetrachord and learn them in scale order as far as B. This should not be an exercise in playing by rote; children must learn to build them up according to the sound, and this is the first attempt at playing by ear.

As soon as these six tetrachords are known, teach tones and semitones to the group. These can be tested while the children sit at their desks using their dummy-keyboards. The next stage is for the group to discover the pattern of the tetrachord in tones and semitones. When this is known, the children should work out, and play, the remainder of the tetrachords until they come full circle on to C again.

As bad habits are so easily acquired, it is always better when more than two children are playing the piano at the same time to make them stand while they do so. Good posture at the keyboard is vitally important, and it is impossible to maintain this when too many children sit together. When a member of a group sits to play the piano, he must sit properly and at the correct height; never with one arm tucked behind his back. Standing at the piano, while the child is young and not too tall, also helps to form a good hand position; the wrists are not able to fall below the keyboard, nor is it possible to play right on the edge of the key. It is also easier to feel the weight of the arm behind the fingers in this position. As soon as the arms have grown long enough to make it necessary for children to stoop while playing, they must not continue to stand at the piano. So often a pupil drops the hand when using the 5th finger, using the side of the hand instead of the tip of the finger. By concentrating the use of the three fingers and thumb only in the playing of tetrachords, the bridge of the hand can be kept up, the 5th finger being used only when this good hand position is established.

As soon as all the major tetrachords can be played by the right hand, make the group learn to play them through again with the left hand, starting with the 4th finger and again omitting to use the 5th finger. Once these are known they need only be heard at alternate lessons, but each time building on the material already known. For instance, the next stage is to play the tetrachords going up in 5ths with alternate hands:

Ex. 12

You will notice that the thumbs sometimes play on the black keys. Children are now ready to join consecutive tetrachords and to play scales shared between the hands:

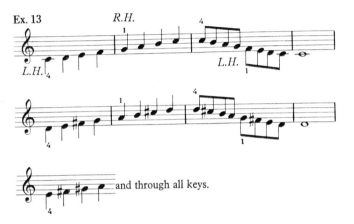

Ex. 13

and through all keys.

You may vary the order of playing these, but start them going up by a tone at a time. For more practice they can be played again in scale order, or going up by semitones. Once these are known, teach the tonic chord of each scale, and let the children build it up themselves by playing the 1st, 3rd, and 5th notes of a scale together. To get all these thoroughly well known may take some weeks, but it is well worth the trouble and later, when scales have to be played with one hand, only the fingering will be new.

SIGHT-READING

As soon as children can read an octave of notes distributed between the hands, you should give them short sight-reading tests. As it is too much to expect a child to learn notes and fingering at the same time when learning scales, so with sight-reading it is too much to expect both notes and rhythm to be read accurately in the beginning.

It is a good plan to make 'flash cards' for sight-reading. Start with an established rhythm that the children can easily recognize, something quite simple:

Ex. 14

Make the group clap this, then show a two-bar flash card of notes using this rhythm. Tell the children to look at the clef, to read the first note, then to look only at the shape of the remainder of the tune, to see whether the notes go up, down, or repeat. At first, use adjacent notes only and no accidentals. Group the children round the piano so that they are all able to see the cards as you hold them up. Ask one child to play the notes on the first card and get the others to make any corrections necessary, as you did in the first lessons. Make sure that *everything* is right, notes, rhythm, fingering if marked, correct pitch, and that the correct hand is used. Children will soon become quick at observing all these things and eager to be correct themselves, and all children enjoy this sort of testing game. Its value is enormous and makes pupils aware at speed of all there is on the card. It also encourages the eye to travel. When children are proficient at doing this with a very quick 'flash', extend the flash to four bars, keeping to the same rhythm. This can be repeated by degrees with new rhythms, accidentals, key-signatures, etc.

Some time during the term vary the lesson by linking the sight-reading with ear tests. Tell the children the name of the first note of a word you are going to play to them, then to listen to see if the tune moves up or down or repeats. Play words the letters of which are not more than a second apart at first, and ask them to tell you the word. E.g. Bag, Deed, Fed, Gag. Another time explain interval distances and tell them you will play words some letters of which are a third apart, e.g. Cafe, Aged, Caged, Egg. This can be done with wider intervals at a later stage.

ENSEMBLE PLAYING AND ACCOMPANYING

One of the many advantages of learning in a group is that there are always others with whom one can play. To start with, simple rounds like 'London's Burning', 'Turn again Whittington', can be learnt individually, played together in unison, and then as a round. Just as children have difficulty in holding a part when singing alone, so they may also find playing in parts difficult; with a little perseverance it can be achieved fairly soon. This is also valuable in encouraging children to listen to one another and to play as a team. (This should have been started unconsciously in the playing of tetrachords.) Just as in good accompanying the essence is firstly for the accompanist to keep going at all costs, and to listen to the solo part, so in duet playing each has to learn to give and take with the other.

When two or more pupils are able to play together they should count themselves in and not rely on you to start them off; they should also learn to finish and take their hands off the piano together. Attention to these details will pay dividends later and will also make the players self-reliant. 'Building-Pieces' at this stage are also useful. By this is meant three or four 'pieces' that can be played satisfactorily either separately, or with two, three, or four players together. This is a natural development from round-playing and is also useful for the slower child who can be given the easiest part to play. In the early stages the pieces would be extremely simple as in Ex. 15:

Rocking Song

Ex. 15 **Andante**

Now that all parts differ, as much attention must be paid to good ensemble playing as was paid to the rounds.

You can make more accompaniments to known tunes as soon as more notes are known, and greater scope for these is available as soon as quavers are understood. It is very important to remember that the beginner will not be able to follow the solo part from music in the first term. To bring accompanying within his grasp, the tune must either be well known to the player already, or be taught to him first. As, also, the pianist has to keep his own part going while hearing another part sung, or played on recorder or violin, the piano part must remain simple, and for the first year at least the solo parts should have the greater technical difficulties.

4 Completing the First Year

All the activities which you began during the first term must be developed during the remainder of the year, but take care that nothing is made an end in itself—all 'ends' should be but stepping stones to new beginnings.

Too much individual work in the early stages may encourage lack of concentration by the rest of the group. You can do quite a lot of work with the children playing together, especially during the first few terms. This has much value provided that it occupies only part of each lesson. Too much playing together may endanger the child's ability to listen to himself; it can also make a child less self-reliant when he has to play alone. Do not, however, neglect individual work. When you hear children play alone, encourage the other members of the group to take an active part in the playing by making them listen to the performer and criticize his quality of tone, his use of dynamics, his finger action, fingering, etc. When you make corrections be sure that you focus the attention of the whole group on to the points you make.

TECHNIQUE

You will find it helpful to teach simple exercises that can be played first on a table. Children are then concerned solely with finger movements and positions, but at the same time are able to watch you playing on the opposite side of the table. A simple up-and-down movement of each finger in turn is useful since it accustoms the child to the feel of keeping his fingers curved and to playing on the tips of his fingers. It is important for you to do the exercises at the same time, as it is much easier for a child to copy a movement, and no amount of mirrors, however placed, will make it possible for the child to see his own fingers clearly as he plays the piano.

You should hear exercises such as this regularly for some weeks until the correct use of the fingers is fairly well established—only then should you transfer these exercises to the piano. If you show children how to relax the hand between each finger movement on the table, it will not be difficult to obtain a relaxed action at the keyboard. You can use any exercises in the group lesson that you normally use for your individual pupils, and these can be played by three or four children together. No exercises should occupy more than a few minutes of the lesson.

Once children are able to play fluently scales shared between the hands, it is time to teach them to play them with one hand. The finger pattern should be discovered by the children themselves, trying this out with the right hand descending from the top note. Many peculiar ideas will evolve, and you will have to wait patiently until the correct fingering is achieved by one child. Once this happens let this pupil show the others; in this way it will be remembered more easily than if you yourself show it, and the child who demonstrated will benefit greatly from having been singled out. This, too, will make others in the group equally eager to shine. Similarly, if there is a particularly good hand position amongst the group, stop the others playing and let them watch. This will do far more for the player than mere praise.

At this juncture you must make sure that the group have complete understanding of scale building, and for some time it is as well to ask the children to repeat the 'pattern of a

scale' in tones and semitones, and the finger pattern of
1 2 3, 1 2 3 4 5 (and backwards) at every lesson. Make
this repetition a rhythmical one; it will be clearer and easier
to remember, and adds verve to the exercise.

Teach first the scales that conform to this finger pattern,
using hands separately until they are well known. Four
children can stand at the piano and play them together,
but make one child sit and play alone afterwards. Children
should be made to understand that they stand for con-
venience, but that when they sit down to play, posture must
be absolutely correct, and you must never allow a bad
sitting position with the stool either too high or too low to
pass uncorrected. Explain that when playing scales, the
importance is not only that correct notes and fingering should
be used, but that tone and rhythm must be even. All musical
training starts with the ear, and it is relatively simple to
make children hear the 'bump' with which the thumb is
usually played, and for them to understand that since it is
on the side of the hand it is very easy to make it fall too
heavily on the key. You must make children listen to the
tone they produce with each finger. Those who are not
playing should criticize posture, use of fingers, correct notes,
fingering, quality of tone, and evenness of rhythm. Playing
scales for the sake of doing so without paying attention to
all these things leads nowhere.

It is possible, with a few exceptions, to make all scales
conform to the C major fingering, either starting on the
key note with this fingering, or on C as in Ex. 16.

Ex. 16

The exceptions, the scales of F♯ and C♯ for both hands, and of B in the left hand, have two white notes only, on which the thumbs are played. The scales of B♭ and E♭ in the left hand are other exceptions.

You can now teach all the major scales in scale order conforming to the order of tetrachords as previously taught. Make the children play the tonic chord at the end of each scale.

Many teachers use broken chords at this stage. If attention has been paid to curing the 'bumpy' thumb, it seems a doubtful policy to introduce now the playing of broken chords which, through the grouping of the notes, makes the thumb accentuate the key each time it plays. Also the 5th finger is used, and because it is a weak finger, the side of the hand is often allowed to play in its stead. Delay using this finger until it has been trained to play independently.

Ex. 17

Ex. 17 can be a very helpful exercise and you should make the children play it in the key of the scale set for the lesson. It can be played by the group together standing as before, and besides being a good 5th-finger exercise, it also ensures that the children have a thorough knowledge of the notes of the scales.

Now each lesson will take on an entity of its own, one lesson a week being devoted to pieces and sight-reading, the other lesson to scales, technique, and general musicianship.

SIGHT-READING

It has been seen that sight-reading can be introduced in a limited way at the very first lesson, and that the use of flash cards later will help to train the eye to look ahead and take in a phrase at a glance. It is too much to expect a child to teach himself to sight-read. Though constant practice will produce a gradual improvement, guidelines at least must be given.

You should explain to the children that a good sight-reader rarely plays all the notes; instead, he gives a good impression of the music put before him, both in notes, harmony, and musical content. Choosing the essential notes to play, so that the outline is not blurred, is what makes a good performance. You must also teach the children to understand the value of playing a good bass line and to appreciate the greater importance that the basic rhythmic impulse has over the melody line.

How then to teach these things?

Many teachers start their pupils off by making them sight-read a single stave at a time. Just as this method of teaching notation fails to train the eye to look across two staves at once, so will it do for the sight-reader. Better by far to start with an easy note-pattern that utilizes both hands at once.

Looking back once more to the first lesson, you will remember that the child who played the simple three-note accompaniment to the song discovered that it was fatal to repeat a note played wrong, or to hesitate, and that by far the best results were obtained when the child kept on playing, if necessary missing out what he could not manage. So with sight-reading, the first lesson to learn is to keep going at whatever cost. Working the music out note by note will make for very hesitant playing. Children should learn to name the first notes in each hand, and then proceed by noticing the shape of the music only. At first it is only necessary to see, at speed, whether the notes of a melody go up, down, or repeat. To ensure that children are reading by interval and not note-naming, make them transpose all the sight-reading they do; be absolutely certain that the children are thinking in the new key. Transposition will be very easy if, to start with, the choice of music to be sight-read is limited to the use of a pentachord in each hand, the fingers merely reproducing the shape of the melody on a different set of notes. If this is carried out conscientiously, it will make no difference to the pupil if he is asked to transpose up or down a major 2nd or an augmented 5th. You will see from this the importance of the children having a thorough knowledge of tetrachords and scales; you should make them transpose sight-reading into *every* key. You will find it easier to go through all the keys if you make each successive child play in the next key in scale order.

In all cases of transposition in the early stages and for some considerable period after, the fingering should remain the same, no matter what the key. You must make sure that children have a thorough knowledge of the smaller intervals, and whatever happens you must remember that 'slow and sure' will pay dividends. Pushing pupils too fast in the initial stages will keep them back later on. It is so important to be content with thorough beginnings and not to look for spectacular developments. If the beginnings are really thorough the rate of progress later will be great.

THE 'SECOND' LESSON

AURAL TRAINING

It is difficult to divorce aural training from any other facet of playing, for all are inter-related and cross each other's paths every time the piano is played. We all know that the pianist has the greatest difficulty in being able to listen to his own playing; many pianists never succeed. All other instrumentalists can play at will in or out of tune; the keyboard player alone has no control over this, and as he is not able to tune his instrument each time he plays, the necessity for him to listen to the sounds he makes is apparently of no importance. But if his performances are to give any pleasure at all, it is vital that he listens to every sound he makes. The pianist must be trained to 'listen' and not just to 'hear'.

Do everything you can to help children to listen. Start by teaching them tonic sol-fa and make them sing the doh chord (doh-mi-soh) first without reference to notation. Dodge from one note to another in any order and any position of the chord until they can sing these accurately; gradually add other notes of the scale.

From this it is easy to get children to play a well-known tune by ear, especially if the first tune chosen has a doh-mi or doh-soh start. For the young child such well-known tunes as (a) 'Hickory Dickory Dock' (doh-mi), (b) 'Three Blind Mice' (mi-re-doh), (c) 'Girls and Boys come out to play' (soh-mi), (d) 'Frère Jacques' (doh-re-mi), (e) 'Hot Cross Buns' (soh-soh-doh) may all be used, and can be played distributed between the hands, the left using the lower tetrachord, and the right the upper tetrachord. When these are really well known it will be found that (a), (b), and (c) can be played together with a fourth child adding a tonic and dominant bass, i.e. the first notes of each tetrachord. It is better to avoid the key of C; it is not, as is popularly supposed, an easy key in which to play, and too much beginners' music is hide-bound by this key, children not being given the opportunity to venture into more exciting realms. You will probably find that to stand four children at one piano to play these tunes together with both hands will be rather a squash and may tend to create a bad posture; this is the moment to encourage the children to change to playing their tunes with a single hand. Make all the children play each tune together first, the weakest gaining confidence from the more competent player, before letting them all play their different tunes at the same time.

As soon as the children are able to play these tunes easily, let them play rounds one hand after the other.

Hickory Dickory Dock

Ex. 18

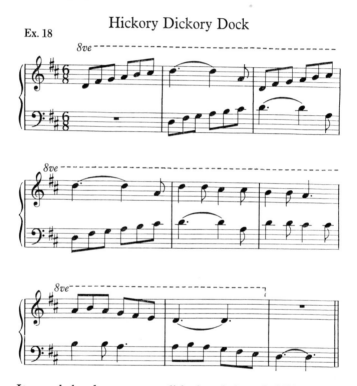

It sounds harder to accomplish than it is and children will enjoy the challenge, though some may be much slower at doing it properly than others. Do not hold up the group for the sake of the one who falls down over this, and as it is an aural exercise, do not use music. 'Hot Cross Buns' and 'Frère Jacques' can be played in a similar way, or they can be played simultaneously, one in each hand.

Frère Jacques and Hot Cross Buns

Ex. 19

Pupils should be encouraged to do this in as many keys as possible.

Tapping the rhythm of a round by each hand on a table is another good exercise that helps to develop inward hearing. Let the children discover the dominant chord for themselves, copying the pattern used for the tonic chord (see page 35). Write the scale on the board, or have one already written on a chart, in order that the children can see the dominant chord in its relation to the scale. This is especially easy if children are encouraged to play the tonic chord at the end of each scale. If scales are taken in scale order, the dominant of one key will be the tonic of the next.

G is as good as any on which to start, always remembering that whatever aural work you do this is a good 'singing key', a recorder key, and also one suitable for strings.

Let children experiment with the use of the tonic chord only, played by the left hand on the first beat of each bar, with the right hand playing the tune of 'Hot Cross Buns'. Let them try again using only the dominant chord, and from this discover why one fits and the other does not. Tell the children to try at home to see in how many ways these chords can be used successfully. Once this is established let the children again see in how many keys they can play this. You may be surprised at the reaction; often one child will be trying the furthest keys with an intensity of excitement that spurs the others to try to do likewise.

In singing sol-fa, do not be in a hurry to add too many new notes at a time. Make sure that the children can sing from one note to another in any order accurately pitched. Choose a key (not always the same one); play the key-note and one other note; make the children sing both and then play both, different notes being given to each member of the group. You can gradually extend the number of notes you use until children are able to repeat two-bar phrases that you play to them. Start by using doh, re, mi, and soh only, varying the order in which you use them as much as possible. Some children find it very difficult to translate sung or heard sounds to actual keys on the piano. This is why only a few notes should be used to start with. Great results can come from little beginnings.

RHYTHMIC TRAINING

Work on rhythm must go hand in hand with the other aural work. Since rhythm is the life-blood of all music, great care must be taken to develop a rhythmic sense in each child.

Many teachers make their children clap the rhythm of each stave of the piece they are studying. This does not go far enough. You must make the group—who in the first year will all learn the same pieces—tap the rhythm of each stave on a table, very precisely all together, and then tap the rhythm of the piece with both hands as written. You must not allow anything ragged to pass. If a pupil, of whatever age or ability, is unable to divorce the rhythm from the melody and tap it clearly in this way, when notes and fingers have to be thought of as well, it is unlikely that the piece itself will always be played accurately. If this exercise is started early enough in a pianist's life, it will develop at the same rate as his technical progress and will not become a problem in itself.

Throughout the first year the group should clap rhythms directly after you without a pause, first as a group and then individually. Music is largely a question of the memory of sounds and rhythms; rhythms clapped by you

and reversed first by the group and then individually

will keep the rhythmic sense and the mind of the pupil alert.

'Question' rhythms given by you and then by an individual member of a group, and 'answered' by another pupil all help to get a sense of balance, and children in particular will enjoy, and should be encouraged to write, a tune based on the 'question and answer' rhythm chosen by the group as the best.

When introducing children to the idea of improvisation or to making up tunes of their own, it will help if you give them a basic well-known rhythm such as that of 'Frère Jacques' to use for their own tunes. You will of course have many more ideas of your own, which you will be able to use in the group situation. It is important that these tunes should be looked at by you at the next lesson, and that each member of the group plays his own tune to the rest. Make the children learn each other's tunes. Each tune should then be played as a round, the children discovering whether the result was a satisfactory one or not. This will give you the opportunity of finding out whether the children have understood the construction of a round. Any corrections that you need to make must be made to the whole group and not just to the individual concerned. If you are a good teacher, you will make this an exercise in which other members of the group suggest the corrections, all thereby learning from each other's mistakes.

GENERAL

By the end of the first year pupils should know all their notes, including those utilizing two leger-lines above and below each stave.

Children always enjoy any competitive activity, and the use of flash cards, with a single note to be identified on each, will quicken the musical wits and perception of each individual, and will also show you if any child is weak in his knowledge of notation. Simple time-signatures should be explained, and understood by each pupil. Try to ensure that these important fundamentals are really grasped by each individual. What is not understood by all at a lesson should be re-introduced with a different approach at the next. If one child has great difficulty, see if another can explain the problem in his way. This serves a twofold purpose in that the language used, and the particular child's approach to the problem, may be presented in a manner more readily understood by another, and the child explaining the problem has to think it out sufficiently well in order to make his explanation acceptable.

You should take every opportunity to get to know the parents of pupils. It is always worthwhile to put on an 'open' evening at which every child plays; show the parents what your aims are and how they can help. Try to obtain the co-operation of the head of the school, keep him informed of all your activities and enlist his help in getting children to play at assembly. It is often a good thing to join two classes together for the last lesson of a term, making the children play to one another. Any activity that will make them keen to get on is a good one. Young children are often dreadful 'show-offs'—cash in on this!

5 The Second Year Onwards

All pieces throughout a child's musical career must give him pleasure to perform. They must also be the means of widening his musical experience and knowledge.

As new technical problems arise out of the playing of pieces, they should be isolated and exercises constructed to help in overcoming these difficulties. One difficulty very often encountered by beginners occurs in trying to make the second note in a feminine ending softer than the first. Most children accentuate the second note in the act of lifting the hand at the end of the phrase.

Ex. 20 a)

Children should be made to sit at their tables, to place the 4th fingers of their right hands firmly on the tables, and then to 'play' the 3rd fingers very lightly, rolling the hands over away from themselves onto their knuckles as they play. This will make the 3rd fingers let go without stress. This should be done very slowly and deliberately to start with, gradually increasing the speed until the hands can be lifted and made to 'float' off freely. Children should practise Ex. 20(b) slowly,—

Ex. 20 b)

allowing the hands time to recover from the rolled positions during each rest. Ex. 21 and Ex. 22 will give practice
in floating off other fingers.

Ex. 21

Ex. 22

Playing one hand legato and the other staccato presents
another problem, and you can give simple five-finger
exercises to be played by the children all together on
dummy-keyboards as well as in turn at the piano:

Ex. 23

Ex. 24

Playing silently on a dummy-keyboard begins to make the pupil listen inwardly to a written symbol, but let them do it sparingly.

You can use Bartók's *Microcosmos* Book I for sight-reading, and as in the early pieces the hands mostly play in unison two octaves apart, these serve to introduce to the children the need for a crescendo in a rising phrase, and a diminuendo in a falling phrase. Here, as in all lessons on interpretation, children will gain by hearing you illustrate these things.

All repetitive and sequential passages in pieces should be noted, and in order to make sure that a sequence is understood make the children continue a sequential passage beyond its printed ending.

Ex. 25 (from Minuet in C minor by Bach)

Repeated phrases need to be treated differently if they are to be interesting to the listener, and repeated notes must lead the music somewhere and cannot be played all on one level. All these things are easily taught to a group who can listen to different renderings of the same phrase, especially if you play them yourself first.

As pieces become longer it will be impossible for you to hear every pupil play the whole of each piece. When you teach an individual pupil, you start by setting a section of the piece to be prepared hands separately; teach the group pieces in the same way.

At every stage it is important to see that the bars of each piece are numbered for quick and easy reference and the fingering clearly understood by all. You must point out any contractions of the hand that may be needed and ask the pupils why these are necessary. Similarly with extensions or changed fingers on repeated notes, all must be discovered and understood by each child. So often teachers insist on pupils using the printed fingering, or write in some of their own, expecting the pupils to act like automatons and use the fingering without question. This 'learning without reasoning' will lead, more times than not, to the careless player who uses any finger whether it is right or wrong, as he has never been introduced to a rational system.

MEMORY

Very young children find memorizing the most natural of all phenomena. Since they learnt to speak, and often to read, by hearing words and phrases, remembering them and then following the remembered phrases on the printed page, small wonder that after a hearing or two pieces are memorized with ease—too much ease in many cases, when children are all too apt to look at their fingers rather than the printed page and play what their memory tells them. Good and reliable memory is a mixture of repeated physical actions, aural and visual (photographic) memory, and musical understanding far beyond the comprehension of the first year pupil, so leave memorizing in abeyance during this time and concentrate actively on it during the second year. To obtain a reliable memory all the facets of memorizing must be used. Physical action comes from playing phrases repeatedly, always with the same fingering, so that the fingers know exactly to which note they have to move. Aural memory is the memorizing of all the sounds. Make the children play the treble melody parts with one finger of the right hand, guided only by the sounds remembered by the ear. Similarly, let them play the bass melodic line with one finger of the left hand. The visual memory, and the aural, should enable each hand to play alone straight through the piece, making clear all rests, etc.

This may seem a lot of hard work, but it is not really. Pieces are short at this stage, children will find it quite an exciting exercise to do, and if done consistently it will lead to a greater sureness of playing later on when the music becomes more complex.

TECHNIQUE

All major scales and their tonic and dominant chords should be known by this time. During the second year, scales should be played over two octaves with both hands together in similar and in contrary motion: arpeggios with each hand separately. When all the major scales have been learned with hands together (this should take about eighteen lessons if a new one is heard each week, and allowing for a few repetitions) you should introduce minor scales. As these children are very familiar with the playing of tetrachords, it will be a simple matter for you to explain that in minor scales the third note of the first tetrachord and the second note of the

second tetrachord are lowered. Children should play all
the harmonic minor scales shared between the hands to
familiarize themselves with the sounds and the notes of
each scale before playing them with one hand. There is no
necessity to go through all the minor scales with separate
hands only, for the children should by now be able to cope
with them hands together as well. These also should be
taken in contrary motion. Some teachers may find these
difficult to do themselves if they have not kept up their own
practising assiduously, but if you introduce them as a
normal part of playing while the children are still unaware
that they might be difficult to play, the children will
manage them in their stride.

You should explain relative minors and their key-
signatures. The way to get the quickest and most lasting
results from pupils is to be thorough in every detail at every
stage. Here again, you will find flash cards of both major and
minor key-signatures useful in testing the knowledge of each
individual. As with all flashes, you must give these fairly
slowly at first, increasing the speed at each successive
showing (not at the same lesson), until their content is
really taken in at a flash. You can use these while the group
sit at their tables; or, to make it more competitive, children
can stand in a row, and move up or down the line according to the accuracy of their answers. Younger children
in particular enjoy doing it this way.

Continue to make the children play the 5th-finger
exercise in all major keys and, using the same notes, introduce a thumb exercise, as in Exx. 26 and 27.

Ex. 26

Ex. 27

You must be careful to see that it is the thumb that moves (especially when going on to a black key), and not the elbow or raised wrist. You can use balls to help get the free use of the thumb. Hold the ball with the 2nd finger and thumb; let the thumb twist the ball into the palm of the hand, backwards and forwards. In this exercise only the thumb does the work: the children will be able to see this as you demonstrate how to do it and will feel the thumb movement when they do the exercise themselves.

To make children stand at the piano when playing exercises will save much time; but when a child has grown so that his arm position is long and straight as he stands to play, let him sit. No good purpose will be served by encouraging a bad position or an awkward one. Once again it is important to let one child, a different one each week, sit at the piano to play the scales and arpeggios alone, when especial attention must be given by the whole group to posture, hand positions, fingering, and equality of rhythm and of tone.

SIGHT-READING

During the first year, children were encouraged to read by 'shape' and small intervals were introduced. Interval recognition plays a very important part in good sight-reading. It is certainly not a new idea but one that tends to be neglected, for many teachers just hand out sight-reading to be tried at home, with little if any guidance as to how it should be done. Dr. Heidseck, of San Fernando State College, Los Angeles, California, has written music specially to train the student in this art,* as has Lois Phillips,† but Betty Belkin, a teacher in Cleveland, Ohio, goes one further, making her pupils play up and down the keyboard in specified intervals naming the notes as they play, and also making them read intervals by looking at the Great Staff.‡ This recognition of intervals both on the keyboard and on the stave is vitally important. However, once the sight-reading goes beyond the five-finger pattern, you can help by making the children say the names of every interval each hand has to play. This ensures that the child is making a conscious effort to think and to play by interval. This will again become certain if all sight-reading is transposed as before.

Some children have difficulty in reading 'over' the bar

* Heidseck, *Interval Play* (London, Mills Music Ltd.).
† Lois Phillips, *Can you Sight-Read?* (London, Galliard).
‡ Betty Belkin, Thesis for the Cleveland B.S. Degree (Cleveland, Ohio).

line, and the music becomes a series of single-bar discon-
nected phrases. To combat this, make the children play the
first notes of a bar with both hands and then place their
fingers rapidly over the first notes of the next bar prepara-
tory to playing, leaving out intermediate notes but counting
the beats. This at least gives a continuity of pulse. Next
make the children add the remaining *left*-hand notes,
leaving out the right-hand melody.

Ex. 28

Ex. 29

Ex. 30

Continuity of the bass line is very important, particularly
when pianists are faced with a difficult accompaniment.
They often fail to realize that a soloist will be able to tune to
a bass line and that the music will sound more of a whole if

the bass and rhythmic impetus are there, even at the expense of full chords or right-hand melody. But as with all things, you must do this in moderation. As children gain confidence you should make them transpose all the sight-reading without first playing the passage in the original key.

No amount of playing and sight-reading, however, will lead to real music-making and efficient sight-reading until the ear of the mind can hear what the eye of the body sees. The sight-reader should be able to hear what he expects to play a fraction of a second before his fingers create the sounds. The best way to do this is to sing; sing the melody of pieces in order to determine both the phrasing and the sonorities required and to get the 'feel' of the phrase. Sing also in as many different situations as possible, wherever you may be. Never be ashamed of the voice, it is the only natural instrument that we have; sing all together if you have a member of the group who is not able to pitch accurately.

As pieces will now be getting longer, it is better to transfer the sight-reading to the 'second' lesson. You should lend children music to sight-read at home now that they have some understanding of how to set about it, but this should never be a substitute for actual sight-reading and transposition at the lesson.

AURAL TRAINING

As with sight-reading, aural training starts with the voice. To hear accurately one must be able to pitch easily. As children have now become familiar with the sounds of the tonic and dominant chords, make them sing the notes one after the other and then in three-part harmony, two pupils to each part:

Ex. 31 a)

Make up tunes using these notes, letting the children sing, and then play them in turn. Much time will be saved when playing these tunes if two pianos are available, for you may sit at one piano and the children stand at the other, playing in turn. This exercise should present no problems and the children will quite easily progress to playing four-bar 'answers' to your tunes:

Ex. 31 b)

Possible 1st answer

Ex. 32

Possible 2nd answer

If the tunes are chosen with care, keeping to an easily recognized bass such as I I V V and using melody notes only, the children should have no difficulty in repeating the phrase and adding an answer with a I I V I harmony. You must do all this impromptu at the piano. When children are able to play question-and-answer tunes fairly easily, show them how the bass parts can be made more interesting; and that by changing the rhythmic pattern of the melody, quite a variety of choice becomes available. Children will readily understand the following bass parts:

Ex. 33   a) Waltz   b) Block chord   c) Off beat

       d) Arpeggio   e) Alberti

The playing of 'shadow' tunes, in which you as teacher play a tune, and the child plays each bar immediately after you, also helps to develop the ears of pupils. Memorizing melodies from sight only, so that the tune has to be heard inwardly and played on the piano only when this has been done; piecing together jig-saw puzzles of well-known melodies such as carols, etc.—these may be done once in a while with the group, and all help to train the keenness of the ear. Nothing, however, must detract from the piano lesson itself, and these additional adventures should not be allowed too often.

Children are now ready to learn some keyboard harmony. Starting with the use of the tonic and dominant chords, children should learn to harmonize simple diatonic tunes, using these chords at suitable places, playing the melody only in between chords. Let the children learn to use three notes with the right hand, keeping to the root of the chord with the left hand at first. When they are able to do this with ease, the harmonization may take the form of a bass accompaniment, which can be varied as before into block chords, waltz, Alberti, or arpeggio patterns. You should see that all exercises are transposed into other keys, working through the key circle the whole time. Only in this way will the chords of all keys become really established in the child's mind. An excellent book for this is *Keyboard-Harmony and Extemporisation* by Kenneth Simpson.* Beware of introducing an inversion of the dominant chord so as to make a smoother bass, until the chords are really well known. If the chords are kept in root position it may mean a lot of jumping about over the keyboard by the left hand, and will make the playing of the melody very slow, but if inversions are taken too soon, children may learn the chords as finger patterns; this is done to a very great extent in America, and the chords as such are rarely established in the child's mind.

Teach the children to play perfect cadences; when these are fully understood they should be played in all keys. Make the children play a triad on each degree of a scale and ask them to find the next major triad; in this way they may discover the subdominant chord and how to play imperfect and plagal cadences. Try again in *all* keys. Roman numerals should be used as chord indications from now on. Write a

* Published by Lengnick, London.

major scale up on a board and let the children harmonize each note using these chords, by trial and error. When they are able to harmonize each note of a scale, show them that they are equipped to add a very simple bass part to any diatonic tune. Let the children play the progression I IV V I in all keys, still keeping to root positions. As children learn the use of more chords, make them play these and cadences in all keys and use them in question-and-answer tunes. From this, it is but a step to get pupils to write a phrase from dictation. Since this is a piano lesson, let one dictation suffice for the lesson, each child taking turns to write a bar. If this is done on a blackboard, the whole group will be able to assess the accuracy of each bar, each child in turn being responsible for making any corrections necessary in the preceding bar as well as writing his own new one.

Many educationalists now feel that to teach such basic chord-progressions is 'old-fashioned' and that the minds of children should be focused on the music of their time and on future developments. While modern music should not be neglected in any way, neither should the classics be relegated as 'old hat'. It is extraordinary how conservative young children are; many find even the most moderate modern idioms difficult to accept, especially children whose early musical experiences have included the singing of nursery rhymes, which establish a taste for diatonic tunes.

Part of the practice time should be spent in playing a folk tune, carol, or popular tune by ear, and adding a I IV V bass part. If you are wise you will understand that this exercise is not a waste of precious practice time, but that the more a child knows about chords and cadences the quicker will he learn his pieces. When this has been accomplished (it is better to do it in two stages; playing the tune one week, adding the bass the next), children should be encouraged to write their tunes down. These tunes will show you how much each child has understood. Any corrections you make must be directed to the whole group; these must be as concise as possible.

Now that the children are beginning to find their way around the piano, and have tried to play a few tunes by ear, test their ability to improvise. Start by playing an ostinato bass:

Ex. 34

Some will be completely lost, but usually one child can produce some quite pleasing result and this will inspire the others to try again. The bass part must be played rhythmically. Even if nothing appears to be achieved, let the children try; this exploration is invaluable even if it only brings home the fact that *some* order of notes and rhythm is a necessary part of music-making. Let them also experiment with bi-tonal effects:

Ex. 35 a)

Until you taste chocolate, you do not know whether you will like it! Children must take turns to play the bass; they may start with a two-bar introduction and add a two-bar coda to complete the improvisation:

Ex. 35 b)

Improvisations can also be tried on a I IV V bass. It is easier for a child to play a repeated chord pattern rhythmically if the right hand plays the chord, the left hand the root of the chord only:

Ex. 36

During the second year children should be able to play 'Polly put the Kettle on' with one hand (a 2/4 rhythm) and 'Oh dear, what can the matter be' with the other hand (a 6/8 rhythm). If difficulty is experienced, let them play the quavers one hand after the other without a break, making sure to keep the beat exact.

Ex. 37 a)

They should be able to tap both these rhythms together on tables, but this is more difficult as the tunes must be heard inwardly. Words may be used to make the playing of two against three easier, but it is a much better aural lesson if this can be achieved without them.

Do not 'flog' anything to death; once something is overdone the interest dies. Even if something is unsuccessful, leave it for a while and return to it after a considerable interval. It may then fall into place; it is quite possible that you were introducing something too soon. No two classes will grasp or be able to interpret a point at precisely the same moment. Always remember that while all individual pupils are treated as individuals, groups need their own treatment as well; you must never lose sight, however, of the individual in the group.

By this time, the children should have played the three primary triads in all keys several times; so now teach roots, bass notes of chords, and chord inversions. Show the children how to play cadences with different positions of the chords in the right hand. Let them discover that the dominant note is found in both chords I and V, the tonic note in chords I and IV, and that if a note that is shared by two chords is kept in the same position, the other notes moving by step from one chord to another, the progression of chords will sound smooth. Be sure that children understand that the leading note will always want to 'lead' up to the tonic, thus earning its title. Let the children play I Vb I; Ib Vc Ib; Ic V Ic in all keys.

To know the 'shape' of a chord will lead to its instant recognition. Help the children to discover that the notes of a triad in root position are all a third apart, written either all on lines, or all in spaces; that the notes of a 1st inversion are a third and a fourth apart; that those of a 2nd inversion are a fourth and a third apart. Let the children find the position of the root in each chord, and exactly how the chords are written and look on the stave. You must also teach them that the quality of the intervals shows whether a chord is a major or a minor one. Too often children have to read up the notes of a chord before they are able to play it; many fail to know what chord they have played. If children are able to recognize chords at sight, it will help them both in sight-reading, learning pieces and in memorizing; a little extra time spent on these now will save hours later. You can help children to recognize chords if you resort to the use of flash cards again. Show flashes of major and minor triads, making the children name the chord on the flash card before playing them.

You must be certain that all the children have a good knowledge of the 'geography' of the keyboard. They should have as much confidence in the ability of their fingers to play the correct notes as they have in their feet when they want to walk up or down stairs. Make the children play in turn a series of notes and chords with their eyes closed. Help them to judge the distances their arms must move in order to play leaps of a tenth or more. Practising in the dark or with the eyes shut will make the child listen more carefully, and in time will give him more confidence in his playing.

Find the time to explain more about the mechanics of the piano; how the strings vibrate, how harmonics are brought into play when the dampers are released, and what causes harshness in discords.

Some teachers will feel the need to teach the use of the pedal before the end of the second year. Since you have been concentrating over this two-year period on getting your children into the habit of a good posture at the keyboard, delay using the pedals until the children are tall enough to be able to reach them without having to sit on the edge of the stool, so destroying the good posture they may have acquired. If the time is right, however, do teach this as an aural lesson. Too many pupils of all ages push the pedals down as marked on the music without listening to the congolomeration of sounds usually produced. A simple exercise to teach good use of the sustaining pedal (*never* the 'loud' pedal) is to make the children play a scale with one finger, counting two beats to each note. They should let the note go down on the count of 'one' and come up on the count of 'two', the pedal going down on 'two' and being released on 'one':

Ex. 38

This can then be practised while playing a series of triads. The group must be made to listen to each player to see that the pedal does sustain but does not blur the sounds. If the pedal is only needed on the last chord of a piece, it is best left out, but if the group can use it to good effect then its use should be taught. A good piece to use in order to teach pedalling is Schumann's Choral from the *Album for the Young*, Op. 68, No. 5.

In the third year you should extend the scale playing to four octaves with both hands together and children should know them well by this time. During the course of the fourth year, teach melodic minors. Take dominant 7ths and let the children play these and major and minor arpeggios hands together also in four octaves. Include chromatic scales and scale playing in 10ths, for these will show you whether the children are able to use both hands with equal fluency. At this stage it is not possible or advisable to hear children playing the scales all together, nor will there be time in the lesson for each child to play every scale set. The best course is to make one pupil play the major scale hands together in similar motion, the second to play it in contrary motion, the third and fourth playing the harmonic minor scales; go through the same pattern with the melodic minors, the chromatic scales, and the scales in 10ths. Similarly the arpeggios and dominant 7ths may be divided out among the group. The children who are not playing will, as before, criticize tone, rhythm, and hand positions. You must take great care to see that children do not play the same selection of scales each week.

This means that you must prepare each lesson thoroughly, and must keep a record of the work actually done. If you have a number of groups to teach, it may help if you make a stencil of the things you teach most often, as in the example shown below. If you put a tick and insert the pupil's name, you can do the preparation more quickly and this will be a record of the work done.

Group.............. Lesson No........... Date..........
     Tetrachords
Play I. (a) R.H. ....
     (b) L.H. ....
     (c) alternate hands ....
     (d) Scales shared between the hands..
     Scales. Major
  II. (a) R.H. 1/2 octaves.   Key .... Pupil ....
     (b) L.H. 1/2 octaves.   Key .... Pupil ....
     (c) Tog. 1/2/4 octaves.
        Similar motion.   Key .... Pupil ....
     (d) Tog. 1/2 octaves.
        Contrary motion. Key .... Pupil ....
     Scales. Minor (Harmonic/Melodic)
 III. (a) Between the hands ....
     (b) R.H. 1/2 octaves.   Key .... Pupil ....
     (c) L.H. 1/2 octaves.   Key .... Pupil ....
     (d) Tog. 1/2/4 octaves.
        Similar motion.   Key .... Pupil ....
     (e) Tog. 1/2 octaves.
        Contrary motion. Key .... Pupil ....
     Arpeggios. Major
 IV. (a) R.H. 1/2 octaves.   Key .... Pupil ....
     (b) L.H. 1/2 octaves.   Key .... Pupil ....
     (c) Tog. 1/2/4 octaves. Key .... Pupil ....
     Arpeggios. Minor
  V. (a) R.H. 1/2 octaves.   Key .... Pupil ....
     (b) L.H. 1/2 octaves.   Key .... Pupil ....
     (c) Tog. 1/2/4 octaves. Key .... Pupil ....

By the time children have been learning for four years they will be tackling pieces of about Associated Board

Grades V and VI standard. In order to teach these well, it will be necessary to divide up one of the weekly lessons, so that not more than two children share a thirty-minute lesson. Though many teachers will feel that at this stage a pupil would benefit by having the full thirty-minute lesson to himself, you would do well to think twice before embarking on this course of action. Remember that these children, throughout their piano lessons, have had the company and stimulus of learning with others. They have learnt to criticize and to be criticized. Much can be taught by continuing this process. Apart from anything else, there is a certain companionship in a shared lesson, and as before it is a great incentive to work.

Accompanying and ensemble work of all kinds should be encouraged throughout the child's musical life. Many children who start by learning to play the piano will take up another instrument after a year or two. Seize this wonderful opportunity, and get them to play their new instrument to and with other members of their piano group.

6 The Art of Practising

To teach a child how to practise is probably one of the most, if not *the* most important part of the teacher's job. It is sad that some teachers omit this aspect of teaching altogether, though they may be completely unaware of doing so. To say to a pupil 'go home and practise this' will do little good unless he is shown in detail how to set about improving the passage in question. If the child is not shown how to practise, he will most likely play the section of music over and over again, endlessly repeating the mistakes, or going back to the beginning and stopping at the first difficulty. This can only lead to slipshod performance.

During the first year's lessons much emphasis was placed on getting the children to know and to understand the content of the music they played; how one phrase balanced another; the shape of a melody; how a rhythmic pattern was repeated or altered phrase by phrase. It is during this initial period of awareness on the part of children that the principles and foundations of practising must be laid—foundations on which they may build throughout their years of study.

What is meant by 'proper' practice? It is the art of discovering ways of overcoming difficulties; it is the delight of experimenting with tone, phrasing, interpretation; it is the quest after the composer's real intent. Here are a few aspects of practising.

The very first attempts are restricted to the learning of notes and rhythm, together with the ability to co-ordinate mind and fingers. The ability to listen to the sounds produced by the fingers takes time, but part of the practice time is spent in learning to make the sound conform to the written symbol. If you play to the children a little during lessons, they will have ideal sounds in their minds which they will try to reproduce while they practise. Part of the practice time must also be spent in discovering which is the best fingering to use, and why it is the best. You must explain to the children that once chosen, the same fingering must always be used if the desired effect is to be achieved. This is vital from the very earliest beginnings. It has been mentioned before that children must know when and why they should not keep to a five-finger pattern. Slipshod fingering in the beginning can only lead to endless trouble later, and if children are made to *think* in the right direction not only will their progress be quicker but a firm foundation will be laid on which to build technique. In the first year the principles and foundation of the practice that will be carried out in the children's future pianistic years must be established.

As soon as children can play both-hands-together other than in unison, their practice study should become more detailed. When children learn to play Mozart's Minuet in F, for instance:

Minuet in F by Mozart

let them first play, in turn, the right-hand notes of each bar
in chords as far as the end:

Ex. 39

Any children who learn this piece during the second year
will not find the chord-playing too advanced for them. If
they have been well taught, children should be able to
name all the chords they play, except the dominant 7ths
that occur on the 3rd beat of bar 3, the 1st beat of bar 4,
and the 1st beat of bar 7. Show them how to isolate bars
4 and 8 and practise these both hands together, apart

from the rest of the piece. Children must be made to listen
to the discord of the 1st beat of bar 4 with its resolution
on the 3rd beat as they play. See that the correct fingering
is used. You must point out the feminine endings of these
bars (endings in which the last chord falls on an unaccented
beat) and get the children to learn to float off the 3rd beat
having *slightly* accentuated the 1st. Help the children to
discover the left-hand stretch of an octave in bar 3 with the
contraction of the hand from the 5th finger on lower C to
the thumb on F in bar 4, and make them practise this.
Children should understand that this contraction is necessary in order to have sufficient fingers to play the following
notes of this bar.

The children are now ready to play the right hand in
chords together with the left hand as written. If a triplet has
not been met before it may help if you make the children
practise playing bar 7 as two quavers first, in order to feel
the beat progressing from the C to the B flat:

Ex. 40

adding the E when this is secure; bars 7 and 8 should then
be played as written. It will be but a small step for the
children to play the whole of the right hand through, though
it may be necessary to make them practise changing fingers
on the repeated notes of bars 1, 2, 5, and 6. In some editions
these two notes are marked staccato, in which case care
must be taken to see that they play the second note staccato,
not joined to the 1st beat of the next bar.

You can now let the children play the first section all through with both hands together. You must teach the second section in a similar manner but the sequences in bars 9, 10, and 11 should be shown, and the children told that where possible it is a good thing to play sequential passages keeping identical fingering for each. The sequences in bars 13, 14, and 15 should also be shown. Let the children discover why the patterns in bars 1, 2, and 3 are sequential in feeling but not exactly so in fact. Before going beyond bar 16, get the children to *look* at the music of the following 4 bars, and by looking see if these bars are exactly similar to the first 4 opening bars. Children should notice that the left hand moves by dotted minims instead of by minim and crotchet in each bar, and see just which notes are used. Again editions vary, but you may find it easier for children to play the right-hand part as written in bars 19 and 20 instead of transferring some of the notes to the left hand:

Ex. 41

Here is an opportunity of introducing the sound of the interrupted cadence, and you should play a perfect cadence and then the interrupted cadence in bar 20.

Children should compare bars 21–24 and bars 17–20; the additional F in the left hand in bars 21 and 22 noted together with the final perfect cadence. Do not forget to explain the 'pause' if this has not been encountered previously.

Some good examples of how practising should be done can be found by studying some of the pieces from the *Little Notebook for Anna Magdalena Bach*, by Bach.

The Minuet in G starts with the chord of G:

Minuet in G by Bach

Ex. 42

First of all see that the children practise the left hand to hear that all the notes of the chord go down at the same time. Very often children play the outside fingers first, the 3rd fingers lagging behind. See that they make the fingers go down at the same speed from the same distance. Show that because the 3rd finger is the longest finger it needs to be curved to bring it to the same length as the others, enabling all three notes to be sounded together. When the children have mastered this difficulty in the left hand, they can add the right-hand note. The children should always say whether they think the notes of the chord were really sounded together. They must listen and be their own critics as well as be criticized.

From the second G of bar 2 the right hand has to leap to the 3rd finger on E in bar 3. If children are allowed to wait before moving the hand until the moment when the E should be played, the rhythm will always be held up at this point. Children should practise moving the hand quickly once the G has been played, placing the 3rd finger over the E in readiness for playing before it is actually needed. You must make certain that pupils are aware that since both Gs are to be played detached, the leap to the E with the 3rd finger is a natural one that ensures the hand being in a new five-finger position. This occurs in a similar manner in bars 4 to 5 with the leap to the C. From bars 5 to 6 the contraction of the right hand, using the thumb on A and going to the 3rd on B, must be shown and practised. Little difficulty will be encountered by the children in the left hand when playing this alone, but before they are allowed to play both hands together right through, bars 7 and 8 will need attention. Here the right hand is in the middle of a long legato line while the left hand notes need to be played mezzo-staccato. For children to whom this is a new situation, a simple five-finger exercise in which one hand plays detached and the other legato will quickly get over this difficulty. Children should play the hands legato and staccato in turn. (See Exx. 23 and 24, pages 55 and 56.) Once this is managed you can make them play bars 7 and 8.

You must ask the group whether they see any differences in the repetition from bars 9 to 16. Again it is of vital importance to make children observe all they can about the music they play, *all* the time. No let-up over this can ever be made, for through this observation and practical experience children will learn more about their pieces, and the construction and form of all the music they play, than from almost any other source.

You will see that the difficulty found in bars 7–8 recurs in opposite hands in bar 12 and finally in bar 15. You will

also have to see that the contraction of the 4th to the 2nd
finger of the left hand from the G to A in bars 12 to 13 is
practised, and that care is taken to see that no break occurs
in the phrase from bars 12 to 13; this must similarly be
watched in bars 8 to 9. All these isolated bars should be
practised by the group at the lesson, for it is in the lesson that
children should be shown and taught how to practise. Make
the group aware of the modulation to the dominant from
bars 17 to 24, and exactly where the music returns to the
tonic key. You must pay special attention throughout this
piece to ensuring that the hands 'float' off at the ends of
phrases without giving any undue emphasis to the last notes.

All these things will be equally applicable to parts of the
second section, the only new difficulty being in the left hand
of bars 25–26 where the music divides temporarily into
parts. Here the thumb is required to play a minim on the
2nd beat of the bar while the 1st beat of the under part is
also a minim:

Ex. 43

You should see that children practise these bars on their own both with separate hands and with both hands together. A slightly similar situation occurs in bar 29, where both notes must be held and released together on the 1st beat of the next bar. Much the same situation is met in the Polonaise in F, the left hand encountering it in the first beat of bar 1 and the right hand in the first beat of bar 3. You must see that these are practised out of context:

Polonaise in F by Bach

Ex. 44

The Minuet in A minor (Ex. 45) affords a great opportunity for keen listening both by the individual and the group to see that the opening phrase of the right hand, from bars 1 to 4, is exactly copied by the left hand in its entry one bar later.

Minuet in A minor by Bach

The bass with the repeated notes from bars 5 to 12 is another good listening point. Children should understand that music cannot stand still; all the notes in a phrase must move either towards or from a point in a tune. You must show, by playing yourself, that these repeated notes cannot all be played with exactly the same amount of tone; in fact they lead very gently to the final dominant notes of bar 12. Similarly, show how the repeated C's in bar 17 lead to the B in the next bar. The cross-rhythms need particular care in bars 20 to 25. If you taught children to play two tunes together as suggested earlier, these bars will become relatively easy to master.

In the *Album for the Young* by Schumann many practising problems may be dealt with.

In 'Melody' (Ex. 46) the first thing to make children practise is the left hand starting on the 3rd beat of bar 3.

Melody by Schumann

Here the hand has to be contracted to allow the 2nd finger to play on E. Children should play this short extract first, stopping on D, the note 'over' the bar line, until the passage is secure:

A similar problem is to be found in bar 4 where the thumb has to play on D. Once more show how this short phrase must be practised on to the next B, divorced from the rest of the piece:

When these two bars are safe make the children join them together and practise the whole phrase to the end of bar 4:

Now they can tackle the whole of the left hand from bars 1 to 4.

You must tackle the difficulty of playing one hand more softly than the other immediately it occurs; it will save so much time later.

The easiest way to teach the soft playing of an accompaniment is to make children play on the top of the keys without depressing them sufficiently to make a sound, while the other hand plays the melody. This creates the feeling of a light touch in one hand combined with the singing touch of the other. In this piece the left-hand part should be played more softly than the right hand. Let the children play the

left hand first with the notes sounded together to form four
chords in each bar:

adding the right hand when the left hand is proficient, and
then let them practise the passage as suggested. The piece
may now be played as it is written. Top notes of a chord can
be made to sing in the same way, and children should
experiment with those in bars 11 and 19.

If this phrase is fingered as in Ex. 51, it will ensure a

legato melody line; you should show children how to practise moving the thumb to the 5th finger in bar 12.

The same problem of playing one hand more softly than
the other will be met in 'The Merry Peasant', in which the
left hand has the melody.

One difficulty, so often allowed to go unmastered in the
early stages, is that of playing two-note chords *legato*,
especially when one note has to be repeated. Children should
try this out in slow-motion first, practising playing a chord
and holding the fingers down for two beats; lifting the
finger that plays the repeated note on the 2nd beat;
preparing the new finger for the next chord; and playing
finger and thumb together:

Ex. 52

This can soon be speeded up and completely alters the performance of beginners' pieces. Quite young children are able to do this easily, and the excuse that the children are too young (and therefore cannot be made to try) is often the sign of a lazy teacher.

This legato chord-playing occurs in bar 11 of 'A Melody', in which the right-hand thumb has to be lifted while the top notes are being sustained:

Ex. 53

I have already suggested that the Choral is a useful piece to use in teaching how to pedal. It is also a wonderful example of the need to play one finger legato while repeating another:

Chorale by Schumann

Ex. 54

Pedal

In the end the fingers should make this piece really legato without relying completely on the use of the pedal.

Children should apply the harmonic knowledge they have gained to the pieces they are learning. In 'The Wild Horseman' they should be able to recognize that the chord construction in bars 1–2 is I I / I IV I in A minor; in bars 3–4 the progression is V I V / I I V:

The Wild Horseman by Schumann

Ex. 55

and that bars 17 to 24 are a repetition of bars 1 to 8. From this it is easy to see that in the following 8 bars in F major there is very little change. With this knowledge it is easy to transpose into any key, and the exercise will firmly establish this chord relationship.

You must show children how to practise a technical difficulty 'over' a bar-line on to the next beat, picking up from the beat on which they stopped:

Study by Heller

Ex. 56

how to practise the same difficulty by starting on the last note and working back to the first while keeping to the original fingering:

Ex. 57

and finally playing the bars as written:

Ex. 57

Children need to be shown how to isolate difficulties and overcome them. Although to begin with this will have to be done during a lesson later on they should be told which bars to practise first. Still later they will learn to discover these for themselves, so that apparent difficulties are mastered before the piece is played right through. There are teachers who think that some of these are difficulties to be overcome when pupils are more advanced, but leaving them only leads to the establishment of bad habits difficult to eradicate later.

These are but a few examples of how pupils may be helped to practise. The important thing is to show them how to select bars that need special attention, and how to fit them into the rest of the piece when they are mastered.

7 The Adult in the Group Situation

As the tempo of life quickens so will adults feel the need more and more to turn to some form of creativity in their lives. Increasingly the individual is being pushed into a world of mass reaction and mass production, and if the 'human' race is to survive man will need to cultivate any creative pursuit that will re-establish him as an individual. As the piano, organ, and guitar are the commonest instruments whose music forms a complete whole in itself, these are the instruments that are most likely to be learnt by those who have left school.

Many heads of schools without music teachers find that even the playing of a simplified hymn tune for assembly is beyond the reach of their staff, and many school activities would be enhanced if someone were able to play the piano just a little. Local Education Authorities, fully aware of the value of the use of the piano in schools, are gradually including the teaching of the piano as part of their school instrumental schemes, particularly in primary schools. Courses for teachers interested in the piano are increasing.

There is, then, a demand for lessons by people seeking a creative outlet in life, some of whom may have had lessons during their childhood and discontinued learning; by teachers, often heads of schools; by VIth formers hoping to make teaching their career; and by parents who feel that an ability to play themselves will lead them to a better understanding of the music their children are experiencing, and also give them an opportunity of playing together. This parental activity is to be encouraged for all it is worth; it brings music back into the home.

To all these the group situation is a relief, for it is comforting to find others having similar difficulties to one's own. Adults are unduly conscious that they are starting late, and in consequence all hope to learn at a great speed, to 'catch up' and acquire the ability to play comparatively difficult pieces within the shortest possible time. It is a salutary experience to find that none of these things can be achieved overnight, and comfort can again be found by seeing this inability in others.

Paradoxically, most pupils approach learning with great humility and need intensive encouragement to get them through the initial stages. Children feel that they have their lives in front of them while adults are over-conscious of the passage of time. The other enormous difference between adults' and children's groups is that whereas the children's minds are like blotting paper waiting to absorb all you have to give them (a great responsibility this, for they will absorb the bad as well as the good), the minds and the ears of adults are cluttered with quantities of unessential material, which will often get in the way of the reception of ideas presented in a completely new format. Children will accept new things unhesitatingly; adults will question every step and will often see and make difficulties where none exist.

Most of what I have said concerning the teaching of children in previous chapters will apply to the teaching of late beginners. Whatever music you decide to use at their first lesson, do remember that it is just as unsatisfactory to teach these pupils notation only by learning lines and spaces as it was for the children. There is, unfortunately, a very limited repertoire for the older beginner. You may find greater satisfaction in writing your own music, but whatever you do try to keep the facts presented in as logical an order as possible. There is no reason why you should keep to the old method of teaching a five-finger pattern that ends and begins with the thumbs on middle C; sharing a note between the hands is often confusing:

Ex. 58

Why not try instead to introduce the group to the whole musical alphabet, starting with A below and ending with G above middle C; the left hand playing A to C with the 3rd finger on A; the right hand starting with the thumb on D:

Ex. 59

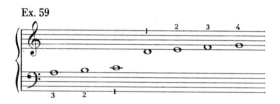

It is better if you use tunes that move only by step up or down, or by repetition of a note, until the pupils can recognize the notes on the stave easily.

It is astonishing the difficulties adult beginners have in merely depressing the keys; fingers are no longer as flexible as they were, and besides the natural stiffening of limbs that develops as the years advance, the anxiety and mere effort of learning produces a tenseness of body and mind; these pupils need many more exercises in relaxation. Give relaxation exercises in small doses from the very first lesson. All exercises, such as raising the shoulders and letting them fall, shaking wrists, holding arms up and letting them drop, can be done by the group together, and the pupils will benefit

if they test each other's ability to relax. A few simple
five-finger exercises at this stage will help to obtain a legato
touch.

The teaching of posture and the correct use of fingers and
arms is as important to the adult as to the child, and you,
in your anxiety to get the pupils 'off the ground', must not
be tempted to let incorrect movements pass by. Allowing for
physical limitations due to age, perseverance in obtaining
as good a posture as possible will help the pupil more in his
ambition to play than will misguided kindness in letting
faults go by unchecked.

The greatest joys in music-making are often found in
communal playing. Adults will enjoy a three-note accompaniment to a song or recorder piece as much as the children;
and teachers and parents will be helped if they are able to
play this sort of accompaniment to a nursery rhyme or
national song. Even a simple tonic or dominant bass that
represents the ticking of a clock would prove a satisfactory
accompaniment at this stage to 'Hickory, Dickory Dock':

Ex. 60

and a three-note bass goes well with 'D'ye ken John Peel'
or 'All thro' the Night':

John Peel

hounds　and　his　horn　in　the　morn　–　ing.

All through the Night

Ex. 62

Voice

While　the moon her　watch　is　keep-ing,
While　the wear-y　world　is　sleep-ing,

Piano

All　through the　night.　O'er　my　bos-om

gent-ly steal-ing, Vi-sions of de-light re-veal-ing,

Breathe a pure and ho-ly feel-ing, All through the night.

Adults find chord-playing extremely difficult, especially the ability to put two or more notes down at exactly the same moment. Before you give the pupils pieces to play that include chords, give them exercises to help in chord-playing, exercises which allow time for the fingers to 'sink' into the notes, and the hand, wrist, and arm to relax between the playing of each chord.

When chord-playing has become more fluid, make the group play another note before each chord, again allowing time for the hand to adjust its position, getting well over the notes of the chord after the finger has played its single note:

Ex. 63 a)

b)

Encourage the pupils to listen to and to criticize one another, for they will learn as much from becoming critical of others and listening to your corrections as they will when being criticized themselves. It is, alas, always so much easier to see and hear faults in others than in oneself.

Adults understand more readily if they have a complete picture of the system being used, so it is better to show a chart of all the note-values and their rests as soon as the difference between crotchets and minims has been fully understood.

Pupils are apt to cling to the keys and are often reluctant to lift their hands from them, especially during rests or at the ends of phrases, fearful that they will lose their way. They will need help to overcome this. A simple exercise making the hand float off a key and descend on to the same one, the pupil looking to see what is being done, and then repeating the exercise with the eyes shut, will prove quite helpful:

Ex. 64 a)

b)

Let the group watch while you play these exercises, and try to make them listen to the tone you produce.

Greater confidence will be acquired if the adults, like the children, have a thorough knowledge of the geography of the keyboard. Encourage them to make the shapes of chords in the air, then to place their fingers on the keys in order to see whether each 'shape' was correct. All pupils whether adult or child should know instinctively the position the fingers will have to take in order to play any interval. For instance the distance from E to G with the 1st and 3rd fingers of the right hand should be gauged; the pupil should learn that, to play G♯ in place of the G, only the 3rd finger needs to move, and the movement is a small adjustment of the finger towards the back of the keyboard. Similarly when leaping from one note to another—from middle C to the A an octave lower with the left hand—not only must the distance be felt with the hand, but the arm must know how far it has to take the hand in order to reach the lower A. All these, and similar exercises may be carried out by the group all together, using dummy-keyboards. Make the pupils close their eyes after the first note of each exercise has been played, only opening them to see if the correct distance has been judged after playing the 2nd note.

It is a mistake to think that because pupils start learning late in life little purpose is served in trying to make them play musically. On the contrary they are very eager to discover all they can about music; even if they are unable to put into practice all that you might wish, they will take special pleasure in discovering the very simplest of things. For this reason, give them as much knowledge and understanding about playing as you give to children. Adults usually have less time than children and prefer to have a single lesson each week, so do less with them in the way of creating their own tunes. The lessons, too, will change and will take the shape more of miniature master-classes, but you should include a good deal of material of a practical nature—simplified hymns, songs, and carols at first. Since there is a wealth of original keyboard music from which to choose, do not under any circumstances use simplified classics.

Adults will not need or enjoy any competitive element in the class, but the occasional use of flash cards to test their knowledge of notation will help them to see whether their recognition of individual notes is as instantaneous as it should be.

The playing of scales and arpeggios is important and you should not neglect these. Let two pupils play them together in unison; with the scales, let the better player take these twice or three times as fast as the weakest member of the group:

Ex. 65

To ensure evenness of tone and touch, hear them played

individually as well, a different member of the group playing one at each lesson.

Adults consider skill in the use of chords of paramount importance. You can introduce these in a similar manner to that used for children; 'Hot Cross Buns' makes a good starting point. You can also get them to play diatonic nursery rhymes and hymn tunes by ear, though adults often find this extremely difficult to do at first. Show them how to add basic-note accompaniments. In this way they will be made to feel that their learning is being put to good use:

Mary Mary Quite Contrary

Ex. 66

Most pupils are very nervous of trying out new things. Introduce these in easy stages and with a great deal of patience and understanding on your part: you must remember that this is a completely new experience for most of these pupils.

You must encourage pupils to sight-read, even if they are very slow. Show them, as you did with the children,

what are the essential notes to play, and what can be left
out and still make a reasonably good performance.

The adult needs to be cosseted, yet needs also to be urged
ever onwards. Pass the pupils on to somebody else if you do
not have enormous patience, compassion, and a sense of joy
at the humblest achievement of these beginners; they have
missed much in life by not having had the opportunity
to start earlier.

8 Hints and Information

A good 'method' is never able to make a good teacher out of a bad one. At best it can outline a course of action to be followed by a teacher, can present ideas and some solutions. A tested method will, however, help and guide a teacher faced with a new situation—such as teaching the piano in groups—to get started. In the end it can only be a skeleton which the teacher must clothe with his own ideas.

More can often be learnt from the mistakes made by other teachers than from their successes. It is easy for an observer not involved in the teaching to see where others go wrong, and this may serve to consolidate different ideas of his own. In order to benefit from these errors, it is, however, essential that the teacher has the courage to make an honest assessment of his own teaching, to make sure that he is not falling into the same pitfalls as those he has observed.

The teacher will probably find that to teach a group during the first year is easy; it will be at once exciting for the teacher and thrilling for the pupils. After this period the teacher must have patience with himself. Technique, pieces, musicianship—all become longer and more complicated, but the length of the lesson has to be the same. Thought is needed and a plan for the second year has to be made. Too many teachers get disheartened when the second year becomes more of a challenge than the first. Because insufficient plans have been made, they panic and give each child five minutes at the piano on its own, ignoring the other members of the group. This cannot lead to anything but disaster and the break-up of the group. At this time it is often helpful to discuss specific problems with other teachers.

In England the Rural Music Schools Association has an Association of Piano Group Teachers who meet once a year* for a course lasting a day and a half, during which difficulties encountered during the year by various members of the course are among the things discussed. Teachers also share their most successful experiences. Many tricky problems are ironed out during this time; apart from anything else, it is always encouraging to find other teachers with comparable problems to one's own. These 'get togethers' are invaluable and do much to help the teachers over the hurdle of the second year and beyond.

Teachers should always remember that each group is made up of individuals, and that consequently no two groups will react in exactly the same way nor progress at exactly the same speed. Speed is quite unimportant; what matters is that some progress should be made, however slow. If it is almost non-existent, the teacher should first ask himself whether it is his fault before condemning the pupils! Each group will eventually go at its own pace, though of course the quicker a group progresses the more satisfactory and exciting it is for both teacher and group. Even so, the aim must be to lay sound musical and physical foundations and to develop really good musicianship at the speed at which the group is most able to assimilate it.

The wise teacher will keep in close contact with parents of children. It is often possible for parents to listen to lessons but, if this is encouraged, teachers must make it clear that there will be no time for pleasantries. Parents will have to slip into the back of the classroom as unobtrusively as possible, make no comment, and withdraw as quickly as possible at the end of the lesson. A time must be arranged later for parents who wish to see the teacher to discuss a

* In the Association's headquarters at Little Benslow Hills, Hitchin, Herts.

particular aspect of the lesson, or who need advice in order to help their children overcome particular difficulties.

Most children benefit from having some sort of incentive to work. At school, a pupils' or parents' concert, or a local festival, will usually suffice, though it is often better to make the first attempts at playing before an audience as informal as possible. While some children always rise to the occasion and, though a bit nervous, give of their very best, to others it is an ordeal. The teacher should make sure, as far as possible, that the first time a child plays it gives a successful performance. A very nervous child will do better playing a duet or a trio, where the companionship in playing gives confidence and a certain feeling of responsibility towards those with whom they play. Music needs to be 'shared'; children must understand that they do not learn entirely for their own pleasure, but also for the pleasure they may give to others. It defeats the object if the child is allowed to dread playing; it is better to wait until he has some desire to share his music-making with others, than to force him to play against his will. With young children it is often possible to arrange a Primary School Festival in which several piano teachers and their pupils join together for the afternoon in one school. At this, simple musical games can be played, dividing the children into teams. One round may consist of flash cards of notes to be recognized; key or time signatures; rhythms to be seen and clapped; jig-saws of tunes to be put together and played on completion; songs to be accompanied; and one piece to be played by every child present. If there is no audience, in the general excitement of the afternoon children will play without fear, especially if no comments are passed at this session, everybody being left to produce the best of which they are capable at that time.

Examinations are more useful for the child learning individually, but it is a mistake to enter a pupil for too many. The occasional 'carrot' and Grade V Associated

Board for those taking GCE should suffice in the early years. With groups, the teacher will often find that the pupils are anxious to compare their standard of playing with friends who may learn individually, and a request to enter for an examination will be made. More often than not this will occur when the first excitement of lessons has passed and the children are approximately ready to enter for Grade III: then by all means let them try.

*   *   *

A brief summary of advice to teachers:—

1. Prepare the work thoroughly for every lesson, making a note of everything to be done by each pupil as well as by the group collectively.
2. Activate discovery learning. Let the pupils teach themselves as much as possible; *you* ask the questions.
3. Where explanations are necessary, keep them brief.
4. Always go from the known to the unknown, and from the sound to the sight.
5. Correct posture and hand positions at every lesson during the first term. This will pay dividends later.
6. Always show the group how to practise.
7. Do not use the dummy-keyboards excessively. Amongst many other wise things, Schumann writes in his *Advice to Young Musicians*: ' "Mute" instruments, as they are called, have been invented. Try them awhile, just to see how useless they are. The dumb cannot teach speech.'
8. Keep the group as such and do not let it degenerate into 'five-minute' individual lessons.
9. Remember the aim of the group-lesson is to lay sound musical and physical foundations and to develop good musicianship. Of the millions who learn, only a handful will ever become professional musicians. The children

who need our greatest attention are those who will never become more than gifted amateurs. In order to enjoy their playing they must be equipped to take part to the full in the music-making of their own communities. Speed is not important; each group will eventually progress at its own pace and not necessarily at the same as any other group.

10. One benefit of teaching is what you learn yourself. Only by learning from your pupils can you pass on the benefits to the next pupils you have. No teacher 'knows it all' and you should not sit back and teach in exactly the same way year in year out. Nor should you use the same music throughout the years. Playing 'safe' will not induce inspiration in either pupil or teacher. To quote Schumann again: 'Regard it as something abominable to meddle with the pieces of good writers either by alteration, by omission, or by the introduction of new-fangled ornaments. This is the greatest indignity you can inflict on art.' Many tutors extensively used by teachers at the present time would not be able to stand up to these criticisms of Schumann's. It is worth giving this some thought.

11. Your method of teaching the piano is your own, but the approach to group work is different. You can no longer sit back and listen, you must take a vital and active part in each lesson.

12. The lesson is about 'music'. It is easy to get bogged down by symbols and technique. You should play to the group occasionally, even if only to show an exercise. Something musical should be heard at every lesson, but beware of over-indulging yourself by excessive playing!

13. Enjoy your teaching!

Appendix

The lists of music recommended for use with piano groups is confined to music which I have used satisfactorily myself in the first year of lessons; there is undoubtedly a quantity of other music that could be used equally well. Because music used by the teacher for individual lessons will usually be suitable for use with the group from the second year onwards, I have not listed music for a more advanced stage.

The list of music for ensemble consists of works that have *very* easy piano parts, with solo parts of a higher degree of difficulty.

MUSIC FOR THE FIRST YEAR
(a) First Stage
Donington, Margaret and Mary, *The Pianist Musician* (Stainer and Bell).
Enoch, Yvonne, *Let's Make Music* (Hinrichsen).
Kirkby-Mason, Barbara, *First Album Part I* (Bosworth).
*Last, Joan, *At the Keyboard* (O.U.P.) (Needs supplementary material).
Last, Joan, *Music Makers* (O.U.P.) (Needs supplementary material).
Quaile, Elizabeth, *A Very First Piano Book, The Story of Tony* (Chappell).

Supplementary material
Enoch, Yvonne, *Nonsense Songs Trios* (*Building Pieces*) (Bosworth).

* Suitable for use with adults.

Lindo, Sylvia, *Easy Solos for Piano* (O.U.P.).
           Folk-Songs for Piano (O.U.P.).
Ticciati, Niso, *Pieces to Play, Book I* (Curwen).

(b) Second Stage

Bartók, Béla, *For Children* (Boosey and Hawkes).
*Bartók, Béla, *32 Piano Pieces* (Boosey and Hawkes).
Bell, Dulcie, *Rhodesian Melodies* (Curwen).
*Dawe, Margery, *Early Classics for late Beginners, Books 1, 2, and 3* (Cramer).
*Duke, Henry, *Children's Minibook of Scottish, English, Irish and Welsh Melodies; of Christmas Carols and Hymns* (Freeman).
*Gray, Donald, *Very First Classics* (Boosey and Hawkes).
Holman, David, *Eight French Folk-Tunes* (Novello).
Shostakovich, *Children's Pieces* (Peters).
Stone, David, *Twelve Impressions, Book I* (Novello).
Stravinsky, Soulima, *Piano Music for Children, Book I* (Hinrichsen).

Music for Ensemble

First Year

Bergmann, Walter, *Accent on Melody for two Descant Recorders and Piano* (Faber).
Bergmann, Walter, *Fanfare for Descant Recorder and Piano* (Faber).
Enoch, Yvonne, *Five Tunes from Nova Scotia and France, for Descant Recorder and Piano* (Schott).
Fraser, Shena, *Five Pairs for Violin and Piano* (Chappell).
Noble, Robert, *Folk Tunes to Accompany* (Novello).

* Suitable for use with adults.

Second Year

Chandler, Mary, *Holiday Tunes for Oboe or Flute and Piano* (Novello).

Dinn, Freda, *Tuneful Tunes for my Recorder* (Schott).

arr. Haydn, Woehl, Waldemar, *Minuets and other Pieces for Recorder and Piano* (Hug and Co., Zurich, U.K. agents Hinrichsen.)

Simpson, Kenneth, *Twelve for Two for Descant Recorder and Piano* (Mills Music).

Simpson, Kenneth, *Twelve for Two Easy Duets for Violin and Piano* (Mills Music).

Third Year and Over

Jones, Douglas, *Ayton Airs for Violin, Cello and Piano* (Chappell).

Strandberg, Göran, *Klaver Och Fela* (Violin and Piano) (Svensk Skolmusik).

Widdicombe, Trevor, *Ebford Suite for 1st Violin, Viola or 2nd Violin, Cello and Piano* (Chappell).

MUSIC FOR SIGHT-READING

Bartók, Béla, *The First Term at the Piano* (Chester).

Bartók, Béla, *Mikrokosmos, Volume I* (Boosey and Hawkes).

Johnson, Thomas A., *Read and Play Series* (Hinrichsen).

Phillips, Lois, *Can you Sight-Read? Vol I* (Galliard).

USEFUL BOOKS

Diller, Angela, *Keyboard Harmony Course* (Chappell).

Donington, Mary, *The Aural Background to the Pianist Musician* (Stainer and Bell).

Simpson, Kenneth, *Keyboard Harmony and Improvisation* (Lengnick).

Warburton, Annie, *Read, Sing and Play* (Longman).